The Art of Falling in Love with Your Brother's Best Friend

ANNE KEMP

For all of the readers who take their books with them to dinner, on the train for their daily commute, on vacation, on the plane, to the DMV....tucking their Kindles or that well loved paperback into their bags to sneak in a chapter when time allows (or even when it doesn't).

I see you.

ONE

Riley

When I bought my car a few weeks ago, I didn't think I'd have to take it to the shop three times in a two-week time frame. Seriously. This is why I struggle when it comes to committing to things. Obviously, something is up with my car selection skills.

"Well, Riley," Dubs, our local mechanic, says as he peeks out from under the hood of the old Toyota Camry. "Not sure if it's your alternator, could be your radiator, but I'm going to need to keep it today to run some tests."

"First, you can't get it to start, then three out of four tires go flat, and now it's a mystery problem." Beside me, my best friend, Dylan, wraps an arm around my shoulder. "You, my friend, have terrible CAR-ma."

Using my elbow, I nudge her in the ribs and bite back a laugh. I'm way too irritated to giggle, even if it is a good pun.

"What?" she exclaims, throwing her hands in the air with mock haughtiness. "Was that not good enough for you?"

Fine. I crack a smile, pulling my lips tight into a thin line. I try to show some teeth, but my lips rebel, quivering and contorting into what must look like an exaggerated grimace.

"Don't even know if I can honor the friends and family discount with that face," Dubs teases. "What *is* that?"

Now, I'm laughing. "You guys, let me be mad for a second, okay?"

"No way," Dylan calls over her shoulder as she heads to the back office, motioning for me to follow her. "We don't do anger here at Dubs' Garage. I think it's a house rule."

I walk into the confined space where Dylan works a few hours each week, keeping the books for her dad's garage. They've been getting busier, so she's been spending more time here, evidenced by her emergency medical technician uniform piled in the corner.

"Doing double duty today?"

She nods, inclining her head toward the desk. "As soon as I get through the last batch of bills and call you a Hitch to get you to the bookshop, I'm out."

I hold my hands up to protest. "You don't need to do that, I have some capabilities. I can use the app and request a ride through Hitch to get to work on my own."

Swiping her phone off the desk, she shakes her head. "No way. Third time in two weeks you've been here, girl. Let us take care of your Hitch because you're certainly paying a lot of our bills this month."

She snickers as she pulls up the app on her phone, taps it a few times, then puts it down in triumph. "Ronaldo will be picking you up in his little white Fiat in less than five minutes."

"Ronaldo, huh? I hope he's Italian and smoking hot." Straightening my shirt, I point my thumb over my shoulder to the front door. "Did you tell him to meet me out front of the shop?"

"No. I suggested you two meet down the block at the laundromat." Dylan rolls her eyes. "Of course he knows to come here. You know how it works. You've gotten a shared ride before."

"Oh shush, I've been thrown off my game today." I pull my wallet out of my purse and wave it in the air. "Do you guys need my credit card now?"

"Nope. Just go meet Ronaldo and his little white Fiat." She points behind me. "Your chariot awaits...or at least, it will soon."

"Ha," I say, leaning across the desk to hug my friend. "I'll talk to you later."

I make my way out of the office and navigate through the garage past the cars that are currently under Dubs' care. Passing by my little red Camry, I kiss my hand and tap the hood, saying a silent goodbye and praying it works again soon. Nothing is worse than buying a car and then having it stop working right after you sign the papers of ownership.

A distant ring catches my attention. Looking around as I step out onto the street, I realize it's my phone and the sound is coming from inside my purse. Shaking my head, I dig around in my bag until I find the thing, then pull it out and press it to my ear without looking. Dangerous, I know. I answer it in my new way because I'm determined that this is my year. I'm going to be a serious professional in all the things.

Well, fingers crossed.

"This is Riley."

The chuckle on the other end is way too familiar. "So, my baby sister announces herself now?"

"Yes, Travis, I do. Now that I'm sinking my savings into a catering business, I figure it's only smart to begin a conversation in a positive way...unlike how this one is going now," I finish, cracking up. "How are you?"

"Crazy busy. And you? Besides being a consummate professional as you keep insisting."

"I'm irked, that's how I am." Sighing, I look up and down the street to keep an eye out for Ronaldo and that Fiat. "My car's back in the shop, I'm late to work, and Mom needs me to have the menu ready by the end of the week for the dinner she has me doing."

"Dinner?"

"She coordinated a charity auction for the local food bank, and someone won a dinner at their home with a private chef. When the original chef who was going to do it had to back out, unbeknownst to me, Dad volunteered yours truly as the substitute. Mom quite reluctantly agreed, in order to help kickstart my new 'foray' as she calls it. Therefore, she's been a bit pushy."

Yes, I should be grateful for the chance, however, I do not want to omit the fact that it did sting finding out my own mother had to be talked into allowing me to do this. I was not asked to do it, instead I had to make a case for myself. Even then, she never confirmed I had the job. I only found out after the charity auction was over that I was doing it when someone called me to set up the date for the meal.

More chuckling. "Pushy, our mom? Never."

"Are you kidding? Talk about pressure. It's my first real gig doing a private event and knowing what I do could also affect her reputation, as she keeps reminding me, makes my shoulders knot up." Dragging my toe along on the concrete, I follow a line in the sidewalk, the old saying "step on a crack break your mother's back" echoing in my ear. I pull my foot away from it as if my mother can see me. If she did, she'd probably accuse me of trying to kill her. "I swear, Travis, I just want that woman to be proud of me. To tell me she is only one time."

"Yeah, I know. That's why I called—I just got off the phone with her. She asked if I'd come back and work with you for a night, to help serve." His sigh slams against my ear over the line. "She was pretty relentless, to the point I told her to leave it alone. I also reminded her that she's the one who put your name forward, so she needs to calm down and trust you. But, I figured if she was that intense with me, I should check in with you and see how you're doing."

My big brother. Always the best friend a girl could ever ask for. A pain in my rear growing up, since we're three years apart in age. But he was my hero and protector, and still is, really.

"Thanks for the reminder to hire a server," I say with a chuckle. "I'm hanging in there. I just don't want to stress as hard as I am. It's a bit of a juggle."

Not that I can't handle it, I think as I step out into the street and crane my neck, looking around. It's a pretty street in a quiet part of Sweetkiss Creek. It's in the business district, but this particular end is also for more industrial businesses like Dubs' Garage. Across the street, there's an old renovated Victorian home with a landscaping company and an attached architecture firm, and a row of businesses boasting auto painting, sign making, kitchen joinery, and even carpet.

"And it doesn't help that I'm late for work and waiting for a ride," I add.

"Soon, you won't have a boss that you have to answer to, my dear, because you'll be the boss." Always encouraging. Again, best big brother ever. "Georgie knows she's lucky to have you working for her, but she also knows it's a pit stop on the Riley Richards parade to awesome."

"You're right. Plus working at the bookstore gets me fifty percent off, so there's that." A flash of white at the other end of the street catches my eye. I can't tell if it's a Fiat, so I keep an eye on the car ready to flag it down as soon as it comes closer. "So, what were you calling Mom about anyway?"

"Aren't you a Nosy Rosy?" he teases. "Something has come up and circumstances changed on me pretty quickly in the last few days and, well...surprise! I'm in town."

"That's awesome!" Glancing up, the white car appears to be pulling to a stop about two blocks away and is now sitting on the side of the street, hazards blinking. Squinting my eyes, I'm pretty sure it's a Fiat. "Maybe we can have lunch today?"

"Today could be hard. I have business here that I need to deal with, funnily enough."

That is funny considering my brother is a sports agent for several high-profile celebrity sports stars. Casting my eyes down the road again, the white car is moving along with its hazards still blinking. It's close enough now I can see the red circle of the Fiat logo on the front of the car, and I honestly can't wait anymore.

"What kind of business is it?" I manage as I step into the street again, tucking the phone under my chin and holding it tight against my shoulder while I use both arms to wave madly at the driver of the Fiat. He's got to be lost.

"Well," he begins, only to pause. "Ah, Riley, give me a sec, I've got a client on the other line."

The line goes silent, but it's perfect timing because the little white Fiat with a man behind the wheel has pulled up next to me.

As soon as he slows down, I step out, making sure I'm in his view. I've been standing obscured to some degree in between two cars parked on the side of the street. Giving him a wave, I grab the handle of the back door and tug it open.

"Hey there," I manage, throwing myself into the backseat. "I need to get to the Pages and Prose Bookshop at ninety-nine Magnolia Tree Lane."

When I don't so much as get a grunt of recognition or acknowledgment, I turn my attention to the driver in the front seat, who is currently frozen in place with one hand gripping his steering wheel while the other holds a phone to his ear as he stares straight ahead. Slowly his eyes make their way to the rearview mirror and he tilts his head to the side as they narrow. Maybe I spoke too fast because he looks confused.

"Ninety-nine Magnolia Lane, please?" Peering over his

shoulder and out the windshield, I point down the street in front of us. "Go to the end of this street and take a right."

Again, a blank stare meets me. I'm about to point out that he could put his phone on speaker if he wants to talk and drive, but I don't have to. He mutters a goodbye and ends the call he was on and tosses his phone onto the seat next to him. Finally, he blinks, nods his head, and puts the car in drive.

Right then, Travis is back in my ear. "Hey, sorry about that. I'm back."

"And I'm on my way to work now." Maybe. Fingers are crossed and the jury is still out, but we are moving.

"Oh good," he mumbles. "Then I may get to see you soon."

"What's going on?"

"I'll explain more when I see you, but I've got one of my guys coming into town to stay for a break."

"One of your guys?"

"He's an ice hockey player for the River City Renegades. A good guy, but he's had a few hurdles lately." There's a lull in the conversation when I hear a beep, signaling another incoming call on his end. "Hey, Riley, sorry, but I need to take this call, too. But look, I'm right by the bookshop. I'll be around so I can say hi before I head over to Mom and Dad's, okay?"

"Sure, but why..." The click in my ear tells me that even though I'm not done, Travis is.

Sighing, I throw myself against the back of the seat, watching the scenery of this quaint small town I live in breeze past.

The sidewalks are decorated with cheerful flower baskets, bursting with vibrant hues that mirror the warmth of the locals here. Antique lamp posts are adorned with ribbons of greenery and swathed with fabric reflecting the season. Since it's the end of March, the decorating committee has done a pastel green to celebrate both St. Patrick's Day and Easter, allowing for a double-dip and giving them a break. At night, the lamps cast a soft glow, creating an enchanting atmosphere on our main street.

Passing by a row of boutiques, I spot the signs for the Sweetkiss Creek Spring Fair, which is coming up in a few months. Another one of my mom's many pies that her fingers are solidly planted in. To say she's an integral part of the community is like saying George Washington was kinda the first President. She's the type of woman who runs a business with my father and has herself spread thin across committees and community groups, helping out and leading the charge to keep Sweetkiss Creek the amazing place it is to live now.

She's a bit of a legend, with her friends all relying on her to do things, but for us at home, she can be a bit of a dictator. Even Dad can't escape some days, but he'll always tell us she means well.

When the car begins decelerating for a stop light, I come out of my tourist haze in the backseat of this stranger's car and realize we've gotten off-path. If this guy is going to try to make money driving around a Hitch, he'd better get a map is all I gotta say.

"Hey, sorry to be a backseat driver, but you're going the wrong way." When I lean forward to tap him on his shoulder, he jumps at the same time a sound emits from the passenger seat that's low and rumbly and a lot like growling.

Glancing down, I cry out when I see a row of teeth bared in my direction. Tossing myself as far back as I can go without entering the trunk, I clutch my bag.

"What is that? Is it supposed to be in your car?"

"It's my dog," he answers flatly. "And yes, Posh is allowed to be in *my* car."

"Posh?" Angling myself around so I'm behind the dog's seat, I get a better view of my no-personality driver. He's huge, and now that I'm paying attention, he looks really funny stuffed behind the steering wheel of a Fiat. Judging from his size, I guess he's easily over six feet tall. And he's not hard on my eyes either, his jawline so perfect that calling it chiseled feels trite. His side profile is a study of sculpted masculinity, and I'm kinda drawn to the rugged vibe he's got going on. There's a hint of stubble on his chin and cheeks, but he's fairly clean-cut.

When I start feeling a little weirded out by my own creepiness at staring at this guy, I turn my focus back to the road ahead. Not much farther to go, I see the street sign for Magnolia Lane. Flicking my eyes back in his direction, I am not seeing any movement that tells me he's slowing down. Honestly, I have no clue if he's seen it, and at the speed he's going, we won't make the turn, not without taking out the flower shop on the corner, and we can't have that.

"Hey." Pointing over his shoulder, I indicate in the opposite direction, the way we need to go. "That way, dude."

A heavy sigh echoes from the front of the car and he hits the brakes. For the love of the heavens does he ever hit the brakes. As he slams his foot on the brake pedal, the whole moment feels like a dramatic stage performance rather than a routine driving maneuver. The brakes squeal in protest, the sound reminiscent of an exaggerated cartoon screech as the vehicle jolts to an abrupt halt, as if it had just realized it was the punchline to a comical joke.

The tires, caught off guard by the sudden command to cease all movement, let out a series of comical chirps, as if protesting the unexpected interruption of their forward momentum. I'm pretty sure we've captured the attention of anyone on the sidewalk as well as any and all of the retail shoppers in the area.

The velocity of the turn pushes me against the back door, my face planting on the window. Smooshed for the world to see as we drive through the small but fairly crowded shopping district. I'm still peeling a nostril away from the glass when Mr. Johnson, who owns the flower shop—which I just saved from full-on damage, thank you very much—waves my way.

Somewhere in the distance, a phone is ringing. It could be mine, but I have no idea where it is now. I'm also hoping the driver's dog is okay up there and not scrunched into the glove compartment now.

"Are you kidding me?" I manage when the car finally lurches to a stop. This guy doesn't even stop in front of the bookshop, either. "Are you new here? I said ninety-nine Magnolia Tree Lane."

Dark eyes meet mine in the rearview mirror. He cocks his head to the side and holds my gaze with an intensity that fills my gut with a heat I can't decipher. Is it good? Is it bad? I don't know. I'm just thankful I'm alive...but I also don't want to pull my eyes away from his.

What is wrong with me?

My phone starts ringing again. Looking around the back-seat, I find my bag where it's landed on the floor and pull it to my lap, digging through it.

"Seriously. You and your little dog should not be in charge of chauffeuring people around." Pointing out the window, I tap my fingernail on the glass. With animosity? Oh you bet. "This is seventy-nine Magnolia Tree Lane."

"Well, at least you're on the right street." He speaks. And a second later, he also turns around, flinging one arm over the passenger seat to angle himself my way. "You know, if I was so inclined, I'd charge you extra for this trip."

"Extra?"

"Not only did you get a tour of the town, but I threw in a little excitement, too." There are bright golden flecks sparkling in those brown eyes of his. If I wasn't so mad, I'd be more into it, but not now. "You seem a little pent-up."

"Excuse me, did you say pent-up?" Huffing, I put my hand on the door handle and tug on it, hoping for some dramatic flair to match our entrance. Only, the door doesn't open. Thinking it's stuck, I try again, only to be met with laughter.

A soft and mechanical clink resonates in the car. This guy and his big brown eyes are still staring me down.

"Child lock," he says with a wink.

I quirk my eyebrows. "I can see the review I'm gonna leave now. 'One star for being a horrible driver and not very hospitable.'"

From somewhere in the front, there's another low rumble of a growl.

Rolling my eyes, I open the car door. "It's totally going to affect your rating, you know."

Ever so slowly, he drags his eyes away from mine and he shrugs. "I really don't care."

"You are so rude," I mumble as I climb out, my phone ringing yet again. This time I press it to my ear while I'm slamming the car door shut. "Hello?"

Spinning around, I'm surprised when I find my brother standing in front of me. Bewildered, I hold up a finger for him to wait as Dylan's voice comes across the line.

"Where are you?" she inquires, her voice filled with concern.

"Well..." I snort. "It's a long story, but that Hitch you got me? This guy is unbelievable. I barely..."

"Hitch guy?" Dylan interrupts me. "That's why I'm calling. Ronaldo has been waiting outside for you for the last five minutes. You're not with the right person, Riley! Where are you? Who are you with? Oh my gosh, are you safe?"

I'm really confused now, that's what I am. Like if I had a title, it would be the Queen of Confusion. I'd skip Princess altogether. Fast learner.

"Safe? Define safe."

Movement catches my eye and I'm horrified, but also kind of proud, as my brother takes two giant steps over to the car, reaching toward the driver's side door. Travis must have seen the insane way this man came careening down the lane, and now my protective big brother is going to kick his butt. There was a time in my life when this moment would have been mortifying, but today is not one of them.

Standing still, with the phone pressed to my ear, I wait for Travis to fling open the door and drag this guy out of the car to yell at him. Ask him what on earth he thought he was doing driving like a maniac with his sister in the car. But no. He definitely doesn't do that.

Travis opens the door, and then he shakes the guy's hand.

SHAKES THE GUY'S HAND?

I'm sure in some other parallel universe this would be a hilarious moment, but I'm so rattled and puzzled that I cannot make heads nor tails of what's happening. My brother and my maniac driver are laughing together.

"Riley," Travis calls out, beckoning me over.

Trepidatiously, I take a step toward the death mobile.

"What?" I snap.

"Meet Jake December, my client and the player from the River City Renegades I was telling you about."

TWO

Jake

When an agitated, pushy, attractive stranger jumps into the backseat of your car, how do you think you would handle it? Me, well, I figured I had two options at the moment: one was to ask her to kindly remove herself from my vehicle before I called the cops. But, I'm a big guy and am known for taking care of myself, so did I consider forcible removal on my own terms?

Of course, but only for a moment. That's just a natural instinct. Comes with my day job. Playing ice hockey for a team in the American Hockey League, I've had to deal with my fair share of players and fans who get a little bit aggressive. Guys usually either want to get a photo with me or fight me, neither of which is something I enjoy, but I'll take the photo over a fight any day. And the women have pulled some amazing stunts to get my attention. The majority of my female fans are cool, but there's the one percent that sends me photos of them wearing my jersey and nothing else. The last one I got was a full-on photo shoot someone had gone to the trouble of coordinating, complete with pads, skates, and stick. She put the puck in between her teeth and it was weird.

But, when I realized this one was harmless and only focused on her phone, I made my choice—and today, I chose adventure. The moment those aquamarine eyes slammed into mine, I had to see where we were going and who she was. It's not every day a feisty, beautiful woman lands in the back seat of my car in a new town and gives me orders.

Now, watching her head swivel back and forth from my best friend and then back to me, I'm really glad I got a ticket for *this* ride. Better than a roller coaster park.

"Jake who?" she asks, rocking her eyes my way again and taking a good, long look at me, dragging her eyes from my head to my toes.

My best friend also happens to be my agent. "December." I say it sharper than intended, but thankfully Travis snorts, turning to me and mouthing the word, "Sorry."

But this one, she's defiant and reminds me of a wet cat.

She puts a hand on her hip and looks squarely at me. "Is your last name really a month out of the year? And who are you anyway to go around picking people up and acting like you're their driver?"

Meow.

Travis's eyes bounce between myself and his sister, pretty much laced with worry. I have a feeling she might be the wild card in the family.

"You know, I considered charging you once we got to your destination, but the wild look in your eyes I'm getting now is payment enough."

"Children." Travis holds a hand up in between us. "Riley, Jake is staying here for a week while I negotiate a contract for him. He's found himself with some unexpected downtime, so he's getting a little rest and relaxation."

Those sea-green eyes flash my way again as she locks me into a gaze. I'm sure she's still a bit perturbed about the earlier miscommunication, but there's a little snap inside me that tells me not to pull away. It's like a snap of electricity: playful and new and really intriguing. When she does finally pull her eyes from mine, that little snap fades away and I remind myself that this woman isn't just any beautiful stranger to me.

She's my agent's sister. My agent who also happens to be my best friend. You see where I'm headed?

Yeah. She's my best friend's sister.

But she is sassy. And cute. But so very sassy.

"So, Jake December is relaxing here, huh?" she purrs.

I knew it. My chest puffs a little with pride as I hold my shoulders up. "Have you heard of me?"

I want to shove the words back into my mouth as soon as they are out. How creepy did that sound? *Have you heard of me?* What a tool.

"No, I haven't." A wicked grin plays on her lips. "Is it a fake name? And if so, why December?" She tilts her head to one side and narrows her eyes, her tone veering more toward playfulness as she whispers, "It's because you like Taylor Swift, isn't it?"

Relentless. I think I'm going to like Sweetkiss Creek.

"It's December because that's my dad's given name." Turning my attention back to the car, I lean in to get Posh out of her spot in the passenger's seat. If anyone had told me back in the day that my longest relationship would be with a French bulldog, six years and counting thank you very much, I would have called them a liar. The only other relationship I've had for a nice long stretch is the one I've had for the last five years... with Travis.

Cradling Posh in my arms, I turn around and face the Richards siblings. There's a lot of similarity between these two, but I think Travis is probably the nicer one in the family.

Riley points to Posh. "Does she travel with you everywhere you go?"

"If I can take her with me, she's coming."

"I hope you don't shove her in a cage and put her in the... what's it called?" She waves a hand in the air as she tries to find the word. "The luggage compartment when you fly."

"I would never treat her that way," I say, cooing and scratching Posh behind the ears. "She's not a woman I'd ever want to cage."

Do I say that last part a little pointedly, winking at her as I do? Oh you bet.

Placing Posh down on the sidewalk, I stand up and cross my arms. "I also don't think it's called a luggage compartment."

She rolls her eyes. "Whatever. Why are you here to chill out at the very end of the season, anyway, when ice hockey games are still being played? I'm no expert, but I feel like that doesn't bode well for you."

"Okay, we're done. Let's not play twenty questions, please," Travis, ever the voice of reason, says as he smacks his sister's arm. "What is wrong with you today?"

Her eyes flick to mine, flashing. "You might have the same reaction if you had someone pretend they were your driver, then take you on the ride from hell."

"Was it that bad?" The corners of my lips turn up instinctively with each dramatic word coming out of her mouth. "I got you here in one piece."

Riley huffs, squaring her shoulders to look at her brother before inclining her head down the street. "I need to get to work, 'cause I'm really late now, but you know where I'll be. So stop by when you can."

Her eyes return to mine, but she drags them across to where I'm standing real slow. Like reeeeeaaallll slll-loooowwwww. Only Southern women who are wet-bee mad can make so much noise by casting their eyes like that, and man, she's good.

Shaking her head, she turns around and walks away, waving a hand in the air.

"Wow," I manage, turning to Travis, who's standing beside me laughing with his arms folded across his chest. "You said she was headstrong, but is she always that moody?"

"No, in fact, I'm a little surprised. She never acts like that. Dad always calls her our ray of sunshine. I'm the one who used to be a bit of an irritating crank."

"Yeah, I guess I've seen that side of you."

"Mostly lately." He shoves his hands in his pockets. "And thanks for coming here to take a time-out. Honestly, I think it's best for your reputation and for your career that you just step back and breathe for a week. I'll get your new contract negotiated for the Renegades and..."

My shoulders slump and a sigh escapes my lips.

Travis cocks his head to the side. "What?"

"It's very..."

"Humbling?" he offers.

"Embarrassing," I respond. "How many people get let go for fighting...in a game where fighting is a prerequisite?"

"It's not about the fight, it's about the way it went down with the Blades." He crosses his arms, sizing me up. "You're going to have to make good with your old teammates if I can wrangle this placement back to the Renegades, you know. When I think back to how you left them, the phrase 'out in a blaze of glory' comes to mind."

I hang my head. "Yeah, I've thought about that. And it's a bridge I'm going to cross when the time comes."

"The owners want you back, but the coach is on the fence." Before I can say a word, Travis holds a hand in the air to stop me. "I'm going to have it all figured out soon. All going well, you'll be playing in the last few games of the season. With your old team."

I'm pretty lucky to have someone like Travis on my side. Some of the players I've gotten to know over the years have had agents and managers around them who are only in it for the money and the little bit of fame they sometimes get for being associated with the right player who is on the rise. But Travis genuinely cares about all of his clients. I know he keeps his roster small on purpose so he can keep things on a more intimate level with his people, as he says.

For instance, how many agents would have taken me out of the city and away from the AHL farm team that had just fired me (thanks, Jersey City Blades), and insisted I come to his hometown to rest—meaning to hide and lick my wounds.

"You're the best, Travis, thank you."

"Let's just make sure to keep your head in the game while you're here." He whips out his phone and pulls up some notes he's made, handing the device to me. "There's a new winter sports arena that's about five miles outside of town, and I've spoken with them about you."

"Cool, man." I scroll through his notes, clicking on the website attached. "Will I be able to practice there?"

"Well, when you're not pretending to be a Hitch driver, yes." He laughs, then nods to a coffee shop as his stomach grumbles. "Before we check you into the bed-and-breakfast, let's hop in here and grab a bite, cool?"

I glance down at where my girl is sitting on the sidewalk beside us. "Is Posh allowed?"

"There's a patio," Travis says, cracking up as he points to it. "You grab a table, and I'll get us something."

As I take a seat on the outdoor patio of the cafe, right in the heart of town, I'm immediately struck by the lively energy that surrounds me. Positioned along the busy main street, the little haven offers a front-row view of the daily hustle and bustle.

The patio itself exudes Southern charm with its cozy setup; wrought-iron tables and chairs, painted in cheerful hues, invite patrons to relax and soak in the ambiance. Cushions adorned with floral patterns provide a comfortable place to rest, while wooden barrels repurposed into tables add a rustic touch to the scene. Overhead, string lights crisscross, their bulbs catching the sunlight and shimmering as they sway in the breeze.

Despite the constant flow of people passing by on the sidewalk, the patio feels like a tranquil oasis. Potted plants and blooming flowers line the edges, offering a splash of greenery and a sense of peace amidst the urban chaos. It's a welcome respite from the noise and commotion of the street.

Waiting for Travis to return, I scan the other tables. There are some folks sitting nearby, eyeing me. My eyes meet the dude sitting there, and he gives me a curt nod of the head, mouthing the word, "Respect." Weird, yes, but again, I'm used to it. At least he doesn't fall in the category of wanting to fight me. Not that I can even understand why anyone would want to fight me, but I guess they see a big guy who plays hockey and they think it's cool or maybe they have something to prove.

And fighting. Not that it's something I want to do, but I use it for the ice. But it's also the reason I'm in the predicament I'm in now...because what started on the ice, got taken off the ice. And then some.

Sitting and looking around the quaint scene, my thoughts wander back to that spitfire of a sister. Riley. The look on her face when she realized I was Travis's client and not the person who was supposed to pick her up. That very look is going to keep this man very happy for a long time.

"Here." Travis slides a cup of something hot in front of me along with a croissant, settling into the chair across the table with the same order. He points to Posh, who looks lifeless at my feet. "Is she okay?"

"Oh yeah, she's not dead. Just dramatic."

Travis sits back and laughs. "I'm sorry, but it's just funny to see you doting over such a small dog."

"She's the only woman in my life for a reason." And a very good one at that.

"Yeah." Travis nods his head in understanding. We've known each other for a few years now. He was one of my inner circle who sat by and witnessed Hurricane Greta and her destruction, or rather her attempt at it. "That woman came in as a hurricane but was downgraded to what, a tropical storm, fairly quickly."

"She did her damage." As she still does. Lessons to all of you budding athletes out there: if you date a sports reporter, think about the consequences. "And according to the story in the paper this morning, she's still trying to take her digs."

"I saw that one. 'December fired from the Blades before May.'" Travis winks. "Terrible attempt on her part at a play on words. Don't let her get to you."

"Easy to say when it's not your reputation that's getting attacked."

"Again, that's why we're here." Travis pops the last bite of his croissant in his mouth before tossing his coffee back. He smacks his hands together, remnants of the flakiest croissant I've seen anywhere flying in the air. We both watch in slow motion as a rogue flake manages its way across the table, floating through the air and landing on my lower lip.

"Seriously," I say, pointing to the flake.

Travis laughs. "Sorry. But they're good—and it was chocolate cinnamon. Holy smokes, the perfect blend of sugar and pastry to start the day."

I grab my coffee and take a sip as Travis's phone beeps. He stares at the screen with a look of dissatisfaction that makes my toes actually curl.

"Well." He sighs heavily. "Our favorite reporter has now taken her fight to social media."

He turns the phone around to show me. "I don't get it. It's only social media."

Travis shakes his head. "No, my friend, she's sharing her story about you on social media now. She's been given the power to be on apps like TikTok and Instagram, so she'll reach a whole new audience."

I'm clueless when it comes to this stuff. "She has a paper. That's enough audience, isn't it?"

"Demographics, my friend. Newspapers are losing their base, so they branch out to other channels to get their stories out and to stay relevant." He shrugs. "It makes sense, it just sucks that she's the one who's in charge of running the sports socials for the *Athletic Edge*."

I'm starting to get it. "So, she can put more things up about me that are negative if she wants to?"

"If by things you mean content, then yes. Anyone else I wouldn't question this, but her actions haven't been likened to journalistic integrity, at least not lately. She's loving the fact you got into a fight with a teammate." He slides his phone back in his pocket. "And a beloved player at that."

"Beloved." I try not to choke on my croissant. "Smoke and mirrors, that guy."

"One thing at a time. Let's get you settled in and start clearing your head, then get you out to the rink so you can do what you do best."

Pushing our chairs back from the table, I stand up, aware that a few more heads are now turning our way. But I'm not going to even look back; I need to look forward from this moment on. You get one chance at a career like I want, and I can't mess up again.

Following Travis down the street, I know I need to keep my eyes on the prize: while I'm here, I will stay focused and keep my career steady. There's a lot riding on this for me.

THREE

Riley

"So, let me make sure I've got the details straight. You got in a car with a stranger, ordered him around, and, surprise, it turns out he's one of your brother's sports clients, *and* his best friend?" Georgie throws her head of thick, full, honey-blond hair back and laughs. She's not only one of my absolute best friends, but she's also the owner of the Pages and Prose Bookshop, where I work right now in Sweetkiss Creek. "I'm gone for one day, and I miss all the fun. Also, isn't that how horror movies start? She gets into a car with a stranger..."

"Maybe next time you'll think twice before taking a day off," I manage to grunt. She can tease me all she wants; it's not like I didn't chastise myself plenty last night when I thought about the fact that the whole part where I got into a car with a stranger could have gone very wrong.

"Hey, look," I say, all nonchalant and stuff because it's time to change the topic of conversation. "They caught the person who's been stealing underwear off of people's clotheslines."

Georgie gasps, quite dramatically as a best friend should

when you reveal a tidbit like that, and comes to stand beside me. "No! Who was it?"

"Miss Pippy." Pointing to a photo on my phone, I giggle. "It's a cat. Seems she's been stealing them and dragging them to a hiding spot in her owner's garage. Says here that her owner was looking for some old paint and found a pile of panties."

"Can you imagine going into your garage and finding some weird collection of random underwear?" She giggles, heading to the storeroom behind the counter and appearing a moment later with an unopened box in her hand. "I would die if I was one of the women who had their undies stolen."

"Not just women, this cat had no boundaries. She took all the undies. At least the kids will probably get theirs back."

"Why do you say that?"

"I don't know about you, but when I was little, my mother insisted on writing my name in my underwear." Looking up, I find Georgie staring at me with a strange expression. "What? Didn't your mom write your name in yours?"

"I mean, if we were going to camp or something, but not just to write our name in them," she says, slicing open the box and pulling back its flaps, revealing all of the pretty new books that had been delivered.

"But, now, you've got bigger panties to fill." She shoves the box my way. "All yours to get onto the shelves."

Rolling my eyes, I start pulling out different titles, lining them up in order of genre on the counter so I can be a little more cohesive in my movements. When I started here part time a few months ago, the first thing I did was to organize Georgie's shelves so they were a little more strategic. Not that she didn't have a good system, but things can always be improved. I broke down her shelf groupings by genre first. Then, while alphabetical is the way most folks stock books, I changed the top shelves so they contain staff and book club picks, then bestsellers in that genre on the next shelf down. The shelves below those are stocked alphabetically. Makes it more fun for us because we get to talk about our favorite reads and the local book clubs get involved, too.

When I bring the last book out, I toss the box behind the counter to break down later, but a small package flies out and lands on the floor at Georgie's feet.

"Looks like you missed this," Georgie says, bending over to inspect the tiny parcel. She rips open the paper. "I forgot I ordered these!"

She scatters the brightly colored contents across the counter. The small pile of thread brightens the mood, both of us grinning as a wave of nostalgia hits. Friendship bracelets.

"These are so cute!" Swiping one, I hold it in the air, admiring it. "I remember making these when I was little. Right around the same time my mom was scribbling my name in my underwear."

She laughs. "I got them on purpose."

"You did?"

She hands me an orange one. "This is for you. I picked orange because it means confidence, courage, and creativity." Georgie smiles, her light-brown eyes dancing. "I figure with everything you've got on the horizon, it was pretty fitting."

"It's perfect, thank you." Slipping it on my wrist, I feel a buzz. Must be how Wonder Woman feels when she puts her bracelets on.

"Maybe you can show them to Jake the next time you see him." She laughs. "After you apologize for being so bossy."

"I am perfect being bossy, thank you very much." I don't mention the part where I haven't stopped thinking about Jake since yesterday. In fact, I've worked very hard to push his six-foot-whatever hotness out of my mind for now. I've been down that road, and it's a no-go. Not now. "Anyway, from what Travis mentioned, this guy needs a break—he's got enough problems. He was suspended from play but then was let go from his team. I remember Travis talking about him when he signed him a few years ago—he's got a temper, or at least has been known to be like a closed book. Very stand-offish, which I can attest to now. He's here while Travis works on a new contract for him."

"This suspension thing sounds familiar." Georgie already has her iPad out and is starting to play detective. "What's his name?"

"Jake December." Pointing to the device clutched in her grasp, I shake my head. "But, don't do that."

"Why?"

"I'd rather not know a whole lot about him, at least not like that. He's my brother's friend, and if I do get to know him, I want to get to know him on my own terms. Not go off what the press or some gossip blogs say."

"Uh-huh." Clearly not listening to me, Georgie lets her fingers do the scrolling. She's a fan of ice hockey and has been a plus-one whenever Travis has invited me to games over the past year. Seeing Georgie, this tiny little waif who looks like a bohemian goddess, you'd never think of her holding a beer that's sloshing all over the place while she screams at grown men fighting on the ice. It's pretty hilarious actually.

She emits a low whistle, alerting me that she's found something interesting. "Oh, wow. I knew his name sounded familiar. He's a superstar who is expected to go on to national teams soon...if he can get his anger in check."

Get his anger in check—and that's why I didn't want to know, 'cause he's still known as the angry guy. But now I'm curious.

"What do you mean?"

"One story talks about how an incident happened in a game recently where he and his teammate got into a fight, leading to his ten-day suspension. The other guy was also suspended, but Jake was let go from the team permanently because the argument apparently spilled off the ice and into the locker room." She winces as she closes her eyes. "Looks like the owner of the team was in the locker room at the time and he ended up getting knocked down by Jake. That's probably why he was fired."

Georgie keeps reading while my thoughts swirl. The same guy who had his little dog with him in his tiny car yesterday took out a teammate and the owner? I'm still unpacking when Georgie does another dramatic gasp, but this one isn't for show.

"You're going to want to see this," she mumbles, flicking her eyes to mine. She taps on the screen. "He played for the Blades."

I wince. I know that team, only a bit too well. "And?"

"The guy he got into a fight with. It's Todd."

"Todd." I choke on the name as my jaw goes slack. "As in the Todd who I dated...that Todd?"

I peek over her shoulder, and sure enough, there's the story with Todd's face front and center next to a photo of Jake. My skin actually crawls when I see him.

Trust me, there's no love lost there, at least not for me.

Shuddering, I tap on the screen and scroll down the page, looking for something.

"What are you doing?" Georgie asks.

"Looking for another story. Anything, just not that. I don't want to see that."

"Well, it'll give you two something to talk about," she jokes, but I'm not laughing.

Todd is the kind of guy who swoops in and makes you feel really special. Does all the right things: invites you to Thanksgiving with him and his family, flies you to a game or two, sends you flowers and makes sure that the vase is not only stuffed with all of your favorite blooms, but that the card is also on point. They always said the most perfect things.

In hindsight, I should have known his personal assistant was the one writing those cards.

Georgie puts an arm around me and puts down the iPad. "Sorry. I know he hurt you. He was a terrible boyfriend."

"That word right there. 'Boyfriend'. It's not a term I'd use to describe what Todd was to me."

Georgie narrows her eyes as she watches me. "Why's that?"

"We never really labeled what we were, nor did we call ourselves boyfriend and girlfriend. It's not like I can say my ex was a jerk. He's someone I dated who left out the part that he was also dating a few other people at the same time." Shrugging, I try to casually brush it off. But man, it still stings. "So, I can't really call him a boyfriend. I think it's fair to say I've never had one, Georgie."

"Had one what?" she asks, pondering my words for a moment before her eyes widen. "A *boyfriend*?"

I nod, feeling a warm flush spring to my cheeks along with a twist of discomfort, a tinge of anxiety, and a hint of anticipation all mixed together, creating a sensation that's hard to ignore. It's as if my insides are momentarily out of sync, reminding me of the vulnerability and uncertainty that comes with thinking about this.

"There's never been someone I've brought home to my family and introduced as my man," I say, pushing past the fact I feel completely exposed and vulnerable right now. But it's Georgie, so I know I'm safe here. "I've dated some guys and Todd was the closest I had gotten, not that he's a winner. We started out and were casual but then he tricked me when he asked me to go to Thanksgiving with him, which gave me a feeling of inclusion. Sincerity, you know?"

"I'm still digesting the fact that you're, what, twenty-eight years old and you've never had a real boyfriend?" She stands back, looking at me with admiration dancing in her eyes. "You're a hottie—how have you stayed off the market?"

"Thanks, but I just never tried, I guess. I was busy in high school working for my family and, honestly, I couldn't be bothered. I was hanging out in the kitchen watching my dad cook."

Right then, an alarm goes off on my phone. Glancing at the screen, it's my calendar reminding me that my dad's probably outside waiting to pick me up since my car's not back from the shop yet.

"We'll have to table this riveting conversation for another day," I say quickly, leaning over the counter and grabbing my purse from where it sits on a shelf underneath. "My shift is done and Dad is picking me up. I need to go over the dinner menu with him for that private meal I'm doing."

"Fine." Georgie cuts her eyes my way, wagging a finger. "This topic is not off the table. Yet. Operation Boyfriend needs a planning session."

"No, it really doesn't," I say with a laugh, swinging open the front door and turning around as I hit the street to look at her one last time. "At least not here. I mean, where do you find a guy in a small town like Sweetkiss Creek?"

Georgie sticks her tongue out at me, but a second later, her eyes light up.

"Well, one just drove right into your path..."

I stop the door as it's about to slam closed with my foot. Kicking it back open, I narrow my eyes and point a finger her way.

"No. No more hockey players."

"Why not?" She is a petulant child. "You can't say you're scared of commitment. You have a turtle."

"I have a turtle because it's low commitment." And Brad Pitt is very cool.

"Do you know how long turtles live for?" She throws her hands in the air. "They are the definition of commitment."

Hearing the word sends a chill across my flesh. I fake-gag and roll my eyes. "No. No commitment and no dating."

Georgie opens her mouth and I hold up a hand to stop her. "And no. Not even one coffee to get my feet wet. I've had my feet wet and was hit by a tsunami. No thank you."

"I don't get it," Georgie says with a sigh, tossing a paper bag at my head. "You're wasting your best years on a turtle."

"I'm on hiatus because of Todd. And no more hockey players because I, like you, enjoy the game and I don't need it ruined for me again." Shaking my head, I stare at her. "Leave it alone, okay? I appreciate the sentiment, but my time will come when it's supposed to."

Disappointment washes over her features, but I stay strong. This is my love life we're talking about. Or lack of one.

"Fine. But–"

"No buts." Waving a hand in the air I spin around and go. "Bye."

Scanning the street, I find my dad's car pretty easily. He's driven his baby, a '66 Ford Mustang convertible. As I make my way toward it, I say a silent prayer that Georgie will forget about our conversation for now and just let me be.

I never even really broke up with Todd; that's how serious it ended up being in the end, or at least for him. I found out he was dating someone else when it showed up on a gossip website. It was a gorgeous photo taken of him one night when he was out with, according to the caption, his girlfriend. I know that the press will get a photo of a celebrity and then try to make more of it than what it seems, but this time was different.

Different because he'd told me he was home sick. Different because he'd sworn to me there wasn't anyone else even though there were rumors. Different because I'd emotionally let my heart get attached to him. I believed him. Trusted him. And he lied.

Sighing, I hold my shoulders up and square them off. I promised myself after that photo and the subsequent cutting him out of my life that I wasn't going to get sucked in like that again.

So, sorry, Jake December. That is why I won't date ice hockey players. Thank you for coming to my TED Talk.

FOUR

Riley

"And that's the menu?"

Angling myself in the passenger seat to face my dad, I fight to not screw up my face. "That's all you can say? I'm starting with a wild mushroom salad, foraged from local sources, and a potato flan drizzled with truffle cream. I'll do a scoop of sherbet to cleanse the palette, before the main course truffle madness, with a sprinkling of chicken, begins."

"Sprinkling of chicken. Is that a thing now?" He winks at me, leaning over to squeeze my arm as he turns down the familiar street to our house. "Just kidding, sweetie. It sounds perfect. I think working with the Porter family and using their truffles and mushrooms is a great way to collaborate with local businesses, too. Are all of the ingredients you're using coming from producers in the area?"

"They sure are." I smile, knowing he approves. I want my mom to like it, too, but Dad's the one I learned from growing up. I used to love hanging with him in the kitchen and helping him cook.

My dad has always been the kind of dad that other friends

of ours were jealous about. Don't get me wrong, my mom was pretty well-liked, too, but Dad always made life fun. And not just "Let's go get ice cream" kind of fun, but fun like "You kids want a slip slide? Give me ten minutes." And, sure enough, ten minutes later, he'd take us to the backyard where he would have set up a line of torn-up trash bags with our water hose spraying across it, laughing.

It wasn't a water park, but it was pretty genius.

"So," he says, pulling into the driveway of our house—our family house, not my house anymore since I moved out a few weeks ago and got my own place. However, to be fair, I'll probably come back and steal some groceries sometimes because I like keeping my mom on her toes. "Do you have any idea when your car is going to be fixed, or do I need to be on taxi duty tomorrow, too?"

"Dubs texted me and said that the radiator was leaking. Luckily, it didn't damage any hoses so it's an easy fix. It'll be ready by tomorrow." Turning into our driveway, he slows the car to a halt and I see my brother's car in the driveway. "Is Travis here for dinner tonight?"

"He gets back on the road soon," Dad says, opening his door and hopping out. "Race ya inside?"

Laughing, I trail behind him. The old guy is always trying to stay active; I just pray he doesn't trip running up the steps.

Following him in the open front door, a feeling of love hits my heart and a sense of comfort washes over me. The familiar scent of home—a blend of freshly baked cookies, hints of vanilla, and the earthy aroma of my mother's favorite candles—greets me warmly, wrapping me in a cocoon of love and familiarity.

Stepping inside, I'm greeted by the soft glow of warm lighting and the gentle hum of family activity. The living room is a sanctuary of coziness, with plush sofas adorned with colorful throw pillows, inviting me to sink into their embrace. Photographs of cherished memories line the walls, each one a testament to the bond shared by those who inhabit this space.

As I navigate my way through the living room, I can hear Travis's voice. It sounds like he's outside, so I peek out the window to our back deck. Sure enough, he's there leaning against the porch rail yammering away on his phone.

I slide the patio door open and step onto the deck, waving to him as I do. His face is super serious—his "I'm working face"—so I know to leave him alone. My hand flies to my forehead, stroking the spot where I've been known to wrinkle my nose when I'm in serious mode. Mom likes to remind me if I do it too much, I'll end up needing Botox.

The door to the house opens behind me and Dad steps outside just as Travis hangs up his call. He waves his phone in the air.

"That was the toughest call I've had today." He rolls his eyes, and Dad clicks his tongue on the roof of his mouth.

"A client?" Dad asks knowingly.

"It was Mom," Travis says with a shudder, making us laugh.

"What does she want?"

"Volunteers," Dad says as he puts a beer in Travis's hand and cracks one open for himself. "Your mother is trying to help get a charity event organized for the local brothers and sisters group."

"Like Big Brothers Big Sisters?" Laughing, I sit back and size my brother up. "If he needs references, I feel like I'll need to step in and let people know as my big brother, he used to threaten to sit on my head and fart."

"Har, har." Travis snorts, throwing a pillow at my head. "I'll have you know, I'd be a great Big Brother."

"Again, as your little sister, let me be the judge of this." My turn to snort as I plop down on one of the Adirondack chairs beside my dad. Best view of the actual Sweetkiss Creek is right here, from our backyard.

Sweetkiss Creek glistens under the soft hues of the setting sun, its waters flowing gently like liquid gold, reflecting the colors of the sky above. It's a beautiful spring evening, and the air is filled with the sweet scent of blossoming flowers and freshly cut grass.

I take in the breathtaking view with a sense of awe and gratitude. The creek meanders lazily through the lush land-scape, flanked by towering trees adorned with vibrant green leaves that sway gently in the evening breeze. Their branches reach out like welcoming arms, casting dappled shadows on the water below.

Birdsong fills the air, a symphony of chirps and trills that seems to harmonize with the gentle babbling of the creek. I close my eyes for a moment, allowing the soothing sounds to wash over me, grounding me in the present moment.

In the distance, is the silhouette of the old covered bridge, its weathered wooden planks a timeless symbol of our town's rich history. It stands as a silent sentinel, watching over Sweet-kiss Creek with quiet reverence.

I love it here.

"I'll have you know that in high school," Travis interjects, interrupting my solitude, "I was known as the most giving student when I graduated."

"I don't think that was an award they handed out." Snapping my fingers, I sit up a little taller. "Considering the fact I still have that yearbook, I can see if that is factually correct."

Travis narrows his eyes. "You wouldn't dare."

Shrugging, I hop up and head inside. "Oh, yes I would."

I've no sooner closed the glass door behind me when I hear Travis call my name again. Sure he's going to tell me not to get the yearbook, I wave a hand over my shoulder and ignore him. I walk over to the bookshelf in the living room, the last place I remember it being.

Scanning the shelves, I see a lot of other memories in the form of photos and trinkets: the tiny Big Ben and photos of us as a family unit in front of the palace from our family trip to London, a book on sea turtles from our adventures in the Caribbean, some photos from the Christmas we spent in Florida. That was the trip we agreed we'd never not be home for Christmas again...not that we didn't like Florida, but we like a snowy, cold Christmas, otherwise, it just doesn't feel right.

Scratching my head, literally, I realize that the yearbook is probably in my old bedroom. I'd only vacated it a few months ago, but I knew Mom had some big plans for it once I was out. I hit the stairs and take them two at a time to the second floor, unsure of what state my room will be in once I get there.

I throw the door open and immediately jump back. There, on my old bed glaring at me is a small familiar dog, eyes laced with judgment. As I open the door wider, it growls.

"Okay..." Looking around, I realize my room feels weird, then I see the pile of clothes in the corner. Looking back at the dog, I know we've met already in a certain rogue ride I took part in just a day ago.

When my eyes land on a suitcase in the corner that's flipped wide open, a little rush of heat floods my system.

Taking a step backward, I keep my eyes on the small beast checking me out and start to turn around. Only when I do, I walk face-first and slam chest-to-chest into a giant wall. A wall that looks very similar to Jake December.

Caught off guard, I start to tumble back, falling into the room. My hand flails in the air, grabbing at anything to steady me, grasping onto Jake's arms and wrapping my hands tightly around his biceps hoping he can break my fall.

Lucky for me, this man is like a superhero and acts in a flash. His other arm comes around to scoop me from behind as he plants his stance firmly and catches me in his arms. I'm pretty sure to the normal passerby it would look like a couple trying to dance, he attempting to dip me and looking graceful in the process, but I'm for sure this loose piece of spaghetti dangling from his hands.

Taking a giant breath, I try to hide my embarrassment and not make eye contact, only to realize that the man's arms are covered in tattoos. Like, not the kind that are too much, but a few tattoos here and there placed in the best places. Skimming them, I want to reach out and touch one, stopping just short of doing so as several thoughts make their way through my mind at one time.

One being that he's just caught me and I should really stand up. The other, that if I can see his tattoos, then that means he isn't wearing a shirt. The smoothness of his skin feels nice under the palm of my hand, his muscles firm, and I realize I'm subconsciously stroking his bicep.

"What the...," I manage to blurt as I try to stand up.

"Here." Jake steadies me and takes a step back, a smile draped across those beautiful lips of his. I want to smack myself. I've managed to check out his lips and find them beautiful. And feel up his arms all in one minute.

Then I let my eyes do the walking. The man is standing in front of me in all of his glory with one of my parents' towels draped loosely around his hips.

He's wearing only a towel.

ONLY A TOWEL.

"You okay?" His eyes are full of concern, his voice husky. I suddenly like husky. A lot.

"Ah, yes." I smooth down my hair and straighten my shirt, my eyes darting around my old bedroom and then to him again. "Sorry. I had no idea you were even here, much less in my old room."

He lifts a shoulder and lets it drop. "Pipe burst at the bed-

and-breakfast so they had to cancel all of their reservations. Your parents offered." His eyes scan my room, and I think there's actual delight reflected back at me. "How could I say no?"

I turn and take in my old space. The walls are painted in soft, earthy tones, creating a warm and inviting backdrop for the room's decor. Tapestries adorned with intricate patterns hang from the ceiling, adding a touch of bohemian flair and serving as focal points for the space. Dreamcatchers sway gently in the breeze, their delicate feathers and beads casting playful shadows on the walls.

A large, cozy bed takes center stage, draped in layers of colorful quilts and throws, but all for sure vibing on the color pink. Pillows of various shapes and sizes are scattered across the bed, including some of my old stuffed animals from when I was little. A canopy of sheer fabric hangs above, adding a touch of romance to the space.

Chewing on a grin, I look back at Jake and purse my lips. "Hope you like pink."

"It's never done anything to me." A smile dangles on those lips like a pair of strappy heels. And why it makes my heart skip, I will never know.

Pointing to a stuffed Winnie the Pooh, I give him my most serious expression. "He'd better not get torn apart by your beast, capiche?"

"Is it weird?" he asks, grinning. "Are you a little freaked out that someone who isn't you is in your space?"

"My old space," I say, correcting him. "So essentially, you're dealing with my leftovers. And it's only going to be weird if you happen to know where my high school yearbook is."

He shakes his head. "Can't help you there."

Glancing at him, I see a small bead of water begin a journey down the side of his face, to his neck where it jumps ship and heads down the dips and curves of his muscular frame to parts unknown. Shaking my head, I give myself an internal slap across the face.

"So, you're in Sweetkiss Creek," I managed, pushing ahead and trying not to look at his absolutely amazing, hunky, bulky man chest and the accompanying muscle parts. "Is it a break for you or punishment?"

"I can let you know after my stay, but your parents have been really good to me so far." He nods to his dog. "Posh, too."

I steal a glance at Posh who sits, eyes are locked on her man. She's looking quite adorable when she suddenly rolls over onto her side and closes her eyes. She sticks her feet out straight as a board and appears to stop breathing.

Leaping forward, I hit the bed to pick her up. I love animals, and even if this one hasn't decided if she likes me or not yet, I can't stand by while she has a seizure or a heart attack.

"Is she okay?" I ask, scooping her into my arms and turning around to face Jake, who is unfazed by the whole thing.

"She's dramatic." He rolls his eyes. "She does that when she wants attention. She likes playing dead."

I look down at the cunning creature in my arms who is, most certainly, still breathing, and I swear I think is laughing at me. I can feel her little body loosen up as she relaxes into my arms. Her eyes open and she begins to slowly lick the back of my hand, her eyes moving between us two humans in the room with her.

"Wow, that's Academy Award stuff right there." Bending over, I put her back on the bed where she takes up her throne of judgment once more.

"She's a bit much, but I wouldn't trade her for another dog. Ever."

"How are you sure she feels the same way?"

"Because she tells me."

"Funny."

"No, she does." Clutching his towel securely around his waist, Jake walks over and stands in front of Posh, bending over to kiss her head. Which makes something inside of me shift, a movement I can only compare to something like a tectonic plate lining itself up before a big earthquake.

A man. In a towel. Kissing his small dog. I think my ovaries just shuddered. Best part is, he's not done.

Jake stands up tall and looks down at Posh, cocking his head to one side. "I love you, baby girl."

In an act of full-on, all-out ridiculous cuteness, Posh jumps to her feet. She mimics his head, cocking hers to one side while a high-pitched sound comes out of her body. It's not a bark or a growl, more like a baby trying to say the words. I think it's what dolphins sound like when they are doing their thing, it's that out of my realm and so foreign, yet it's also so amazing.

When she's done, Jake turns around to face me, a smirk on his face. He gives a little nod and does a quick bow at the waist. "And that is how you get your dog to talk to you."

"Okay, well, that is exceptional." There's a weird flutter inside me as I hold up the yearbook and wave it in the air. "My mission is accomplished. I'm wanted on the deck."

Jake looks down at the towel, and of course, my eyes go with his. No, no, no.

"I should get changed," he says, inclining his head toward the room behind me. "And look, I'm sorry about the other day. I should have said something, but..."

"It's fine." I wave it off like I'm chill right now. So chill. And not freaking out inside that this man is actually extremely cool and seems to have a wicked sense of humor. And he has abs I swear I could bounce a quarter off. My eyes keep trying to look their way, but I'm fighting a good fight here and working really hard so they won't go off on their own and do what they want. Stupid eyes.

Yet, those big brown eyes of his pull me in, like a fish that's been hooked on a line. He runs his fingers through his hair. "Maybe I'll see you again?"

The actual thought of seeing him again sends a wild thrill through my semi-irritated system. I really have no reason to be irritated at this point, in fact, I feel like asking why he got into such a huge fight with my ex.

Look, I'm not a girl that is gonna condone fighting, but even I know that in hockey sometimes it's necessary. And also in affairs of the heart, so the fact that he is the man who fought someone who was so horrible to me makes Jake more intriguing. Do I want to do a deep dive of my own and go home and let my fingers do the Googling? You bet.

And the flutter that is currently flitting about my tummy isn't helping me. Not one bit. Not when I can't stop looking into those dark brown eyes of his and wonder why they look so sad. The urge to reach out and touch his arm is back, and it takes all I have inside me to not smack that arm with the other one. I've been around this man only a couple of times now, and he's turning my radar upside down. Oh, except for the part where there is this feeling of a hook in my very core and it's tugging me into him.

This internal battle I'm having can only mean one thing.

But. No.

No, no, no! There's a little voice inside my head that starts to get very loud. Like, super loud.

NO MORE HOCKEY PLAYERS, RILEY! it screams.

I should listen to it.

"Yeah, maybe." Swallowing, I step backward, smacking into the doorjamb. Cursing his sorcery under my breath, my eyes find him and there's laughter dancing behind them. I'm not smooth at the best of times, so I am well aware I'm not making any kind of graceful impressions now.

Despite his best hypnotic efforts, I finally pull my eyes from the tractor beam that is Jake. Taking a step to the right, I all but fall into the hallway and break free of the room.

As I head back down the stairs, quickly, my mind is already turning its gears, wondering why. Why am I feeling like a girl in high school with a crush? Why is my heart slamming in my chest? Besides the part where he was wearing only a towel, it was just a run-in with some guy who happens to be staying in my old bedroom. But also, why care about seeing him again? I don't need to and, in fact, it's probably better that I steer clear of my parents' house until he's gone.

Jake is only here for a little bit longer. What's the saying, here for a good time and not a long one...?

Right?

FIVE

Jake

Stepping onto the ice rink early in the morning, before the sun has fully risen, there's a stillness that envelops the entire arena. The only sound is the faint hum of the ice resurfacer as it glides across the surface, smoothing out any imperfections left from the previous day's activities. The air is crisp and cold, tinged with the promise of a brand-new day.

I've always liked this time of day to be on a rink. The ice stretches out before me, pristine and untouched, like a blank canvas waiting to be painted. It's a moment of quiet solitude, a rare opportunity for reflection before the chaos of the day begins.

I take a deep breath, the chill of the air filling my lungs as I skate out onto the ice. The blades of my skates bite into the surface with a satisfying crunch, sending a shiver of anticipation down my spine. This is my sanctuary, my home away from home, where the world fades away and it's just me and the ice.

As I glide effortlessly across the rink, I can't help but feel a sense of peace wash over me. The rhythmic sound of my skates cutting through the ice is like music to my ears, a familiar melody that soothes my soul. This is my playground. It's definitely not as big as the one we use for the Renegades, but it's perfect for what I need right now.

I love the feeling that rushes through me as soon as my blades hit the ice; I am in control and feel like I have a superpower that no one can take away from me.

Travis said he'd called ahead and arranged for someone to set up the ice for me today to give me a good run at some drills I'm used to doing. When I arrived, one of the guys who runs the concession stand had placed small black circular objects that look like riding lawn mower tires in strategic places around the ice. Not what I'm used to, but it works.

I toss a puck in front of me as I step onto the ice and start the first of my drills—doing tight turns around those tires for puck protection. The ambient noise of the air conditioning, the glide of the blades of my skates on the ice, topped off with the sound of the puck as my stick taps it every few seconds releases any tension I've been holding in my shoulders.

I stay working on this move for another few minutes before flowing into pivot practice, using my body to provide cover and pivot while making sure the puck is protected. My dad pops into my thoughts again; he's not had it easy for the last few years, but I'm proud of the man he wants to be. One of the perks of playing for a team is the steady paycheck, and Travis has been good about handling my negotiations so I get fair pay, and it helps me to take care of my dad, too.

I move onto inside-out pivots now, and the drills get more complex—kind of like that father-son relationship. Just thinking about the last time I saw him, I can feel my energy get more chaotic, frenetic, and I know I need to work on this. I can't let my worry for him spark an internal rage that starts to show; it'll just make people think they're right about me.

It's not that I'm angry at my pops, it's that I'm angry at

the situation. My mother died when I was little, so it was him doing the best he could for us, and on a meager restaurant manager's salary. When I wanted to start playing ice hockey, he took a second job on the weekends working as a waiter for an early breakfast shift so he'd make enough money to pay for my gear.

We didn't have a lot, but he always made sure we were never lacking. He always put me first, and I'll be repaying him for that for the rest of our lives.

I stay focused and work on more drills, coming out of my little world of solace when I notice more people are in the arena now. Slowing down, I stop near the edge to catch my breath and look around.

"Um, excuse me," someone calls out, "but I think my son's team needs the ice now."

Spinning around, I find a tall woman with blond hair piled high on top of her head and sunglasses pushed back watching me with a sparkle in her eye as she leans against the balustrade. A little knock in my gut tells me I've seen that look before, but I'm going to give her the benefit of the doubt.

"Oh?" I skate over to a stop just beyond where she's standing. As I do, she makes sure I see as she gives a look, sweeping her eyes up one side of my body and right back down the other. "I think I have it until ten."

"It's nine-fifty now, so..." She taps her wrist and winks at me. When I look closer, she's not even wearing a watch.

"Gotcha." Skating backward, I start picking up the tiny tires and bringing them over to the side of the rink, tossing them over the balustrade to get them off the ice.

"I'd help you if I could," she all but purrs. When I look her way, she makes a little show out of taking her hair out of its bun and shakes her head like she's a shampoo model, then lets it hang loose around her face. She's a beautiful woman, but the way she's just angled her body at me and the expression she wears tells me she's one of "those" fans.

For the record, I love my fans; I've got some amazing folks who support me, but there's a small percentage who do things like send me their undergarments in the mail or show up at games in my jersey and try to break into the locker room so they can meet me. Both of these are true stories and not events I'd like to repeat.

"It's totally fine," I mumble, trying not to make eye contact like you're supposed to do with bears. I saw a documentary on black bears once, which said if you're in the wild and you see one, do not make eye contact because they see it as a challenge. Of course, my mind stored that very valuable piece of information away for my next outing around bears.

I skate over to the exit and come off the ice to get my phone so I can call for a ride, and she follows me. Great. I can see my future now: for at least the next thirty minutes, I'll be hiding out in the locker room until my ride gets here.

"You must be new in town," she says, sidestepping a small gang of kids who are horsing around as they pull on their gear. "I'm Mandy. My son plays in the junior league."

"That's nice, I hope he likes it." I can be kind and professional while moving at a swift pace, but she's keeping up.

"He could use some private lessons. Know anyone who may be able to help?"

"Mandy, I can think of about ten guys who could help you out," a familiar voice calls out. "In fact, one of them is your husband. Isn't he the coach of your son's team?"

When I look toward the voice, a warmth floods my veins and my stomach dips. Said dip is followed by a tingling feeling that rolls right across my body.

Can't lie—it's pretty interesting to watch Mandy's eyes narrow as she sets her sights on Riley.

"Hi, Riley," she says with venom dripping from each word. "Nice to see you."

"Sure it is." Riley laughs. She shifts her weight from one foot to the other to balance out the giant brown box she's busy balancing. "How are things going with planning for the fundraiser?"

"Good," she says, flicking her hand toward me. "In fact, I had an idea to ask this superstar if he'd be so kind as to donate something to the event."

Riley's eyes meet mine and she makes a face as she rolls them. It's like she's reading my mind.

"Well, run it past my mom first, okay? We both know how much of a control freak she can be. She likes handling all the requests for items to be donated for any event she does, so I'm sure she'll want to handle this one with Jake as well."

Mandy purses her lips tightly, her gaze swinging back and forth between Riley and me until she busies herself pulling her hair back up into a pile on top of her head.

"Thanks for the tip, Riley," she growls as she walks off, turning around one last time to smirk in my direction. "And I'll see you around."

We both watch her walk away, joining a small crowd of parents on the other side of the rink as they settle in to watch their kids practice. When I turn to Riley, she's chewing her cheek.

"You think it's funny?"

"She's always been a nightmare. She drives everyone crazy." Riley stands with her hand on her hip, head tilted to the side, and is one hundred percent sizing me up right now. "Have you ever seen *Dirty Dancing*?"

"I have."

"Well, do you remember the woman who Johnny would give dancing lessons to, the one whose husband never paid her any attention? She was sleeping with Johnny and I think some of the other employees at the summer lodge thing they were staying at."

"I think we saw her leave the cabin of the guy who got her sister pregnant, right?"

Riley's eyes widen and she steps back, nodding with approval. "Okay, you know your movie trivia."

"It's *Dirty Dancing*," I say with a wink. "It's like a prerequisite to watch when you're a teenager."

She giggles and it makes me smile wider. "Well, that's her. She does mean well, but she's perpetually in heat."

A hot flush makes its way across my cheeks. "Okay, then. Noted."

She looks around the arena, scanning the groups of people who are milling about before her eyes land on me again. "Just trying to be helpful."

"Well," I tease, standing up. I hold my hands out to my side. "If you're here hoping to catch a ride, I'm closed today. You'll have to call a cab."

"You know, you're the one who let a stranger in a strange town get in your car." She rolls her eyes. "And I thought we've moved past that."

"Your argument may be factually correct, but also makes no sense." Wagging a finger, I step closer to her, getting a whiff of gardenia and lilies, which I know ain't me. "By calling a shared ride, using an app, you are taking a risk because how do you know whose car you're getting into? You could, I don't know...hop into the wrong car by mistake?"

I know my point is made by the flush of pink spreading across her cheeks.

"Whatever." She holds up her box in the air and starts backing away. "I need to drop this off and go. Do you need my security services any longer?"

"No, but I'd love to know what you've got in that box."

"Croissants." A shy smile flits across her lips.

"You're a baker?"

"I just happen to make a croissant that the locals would kill for, or so I've been told," she says with a giggle. "I'm doing it to help pay the bills while I get my catering business off the ground."

I reach toward the box, but she moves her body so it's out of reach. "Sorry, but you'll have to pay for one at the concession stand like everyone else."

"Fine." I sit down and start taking off my skates. "I'll do that."

"Good. Well, you do what you need and I'll go back to work. See you around, December," she says over her shoulder as she heads over to the stand.

Once my skates are off, I make my way to the locker room to change, coming back out a few minutes later only to find someone's waiting for me at the locker room door.

"Hey, there," Mandy says, placing a hand on my arm to stop me. "You know, I was serious. About the lessons."

A nervous heat flows through me. It's one thing when a single fan does this to you, but now that I know she's married with kids and both her husband and son are here, I just feel icky.

"Sorry, I don't do lessons," I say, pushing past her. Glancing around, my eyes land on Riley, who is still standing at the counter talking to one of the guys who works here. I still have my iPhone clutched in my hand to call her dad for a ride, but judging the predatory way I'm being stalked, I need to get out of here now.

"I'll make it worth your while," Mandy says, her voice lower. "They'd be for my son and for me, too."

We're getting closer to the stand, and I can't move fast enough. It feels like time is standing still and not in a good way. I want to get far away from this and fast.

"Sorry, Mandy, I can't. I need to...Riley!" I call out as I jog toward Riley, who turns at what I assume is the sound of her name. I throw my hand in the air and wave as I get closer.

I'm going to the sidebar here to let you know I'm a very smooth man when I'm on the ice. I can skate like nobody's business, like a fish to water. Me and my skates. Graceful. But today, me and walking? We're failing to communicate.

Something happens as I get closer to Riley. My feet stop talking with my brain, or vice versa. All I know is that they suddenly trip up, and in a classic case of Murphy's Law, I'm about to bite it.

I'm a big guy, so I know if I go down, it's going to hurt. But if I go down and take someone out with me, I could also hurt them. All of this races through my mind as I find myself blindly reaching out, swiping and accidentally grabbing Riley. She's now been pulled into my tornado and is along for the ride whether she likes it or not.

In one swift and smooth—if I do say so myself—move, I manage to deftly turn myself around in midair as I'm falling to the ground so I can place myself squarely between her and the concrete floor.

One giant thud later, and we're a tangled mess of limbs. I can't see anything, but I feel her weight on top of my body, and her hair is in my mouth. She smells like flowers and lime, with a hint of happiness and sunshine. I can feel the warmth of her body against mine and it feels like a soft blanket on a cold day. Perfection.

Is it weird I want to savor this moment for just a hot second before it ends?

As she rolls over, her eyes wide, Riley shakes her head. "If you needed to get my attention, you could have just said my name, Twinkletoes."

"I do have a favor I wanted to ask."

Eyes full of laughter find mine. "More security?"

"Can I get a ride?"

SIX

Riley

Being in the same room as Jake December can be one thing, especially now that I've seen him, his tattoos, and his ridiculously delicious muscles in all of the best places wrapped like a Christmas present in a fluffy towel—

But being in a small space like the front seat of a car with him? Well, that's a whole other story altogether. At least now that I know him it is.

I'm shocked at my own actions when I realize I'm sneaking sideways glances at him as I drive us along back roads to my parents' house.

"Are you checking me out, Richards?" His voice is literally smooth like velvet. Like a velvety hot chocolate on a winter's night.

And this girl is thirsty.

"Nope." Keeping my eye focused on the road ahead, I give a little head nod in the direction I'm driving. "I'm a one-way kind of gal. Focusing on one thing at a time."

"A one-way kind of gal, huh?" he asks, his tone teasing.

"Just, shush," I say, laughing. "And also, enjoy the payback of getting a ride with a stranger. I should drive like a bat out of hell and freak you out the whole way back."

"But you're not a stranger anymore, are you?" He pokes my shoulder with one finger playfully. "You're Travis's little sister."

"That I am." This man smells like sweat, clean sheets, and sandalwood. Why in the world is that combination even appealing to me right now? "He said you're his best friend."

Jake nods, shifting in his seat a little. "Your brother has been good to me over the years. We were friends before I signed with him."

"Friends first, huh?" I can't hide the grin that plays on my lips. "You know, our parents always said that the best relationships start that way. It's how their love story started."

"Well, to be fair, he's not really my type." He leans across the seat, closer to me. "He's a little more intense than I usually date."

"Fair enough," I say with a chuckle, slowing to turn down my old street.

"So, the croissants," Jake says slowly, drawing out each word so its syllables are longer than ever.

Narrowing my eyes, I throw a look in his direction. "What about them?"

"They're really good. Are you going to open a bakery?"

"Me? No way. This is something I'm doing to help bring in extra cash right now. I want to be a personal chef—cater private functions and work with people on meal delivery. I've got a one-year plan. I'm in my testing and practice mode now."

"One-year plan?"

Turning into the driveway of my former home, I kill the ignition and turn in my seat to face Jake. He has boy-next-door vibes happening right now like nobody's business. My stomach dips as my eyes lock with his.

"This year, I'm putting myself out there and working on both larger functions that I can cater while I also hone my personal chef skills. Mostly on friends at the moment." Movement from the house catches my eye, and I look up to see my mother standing in the front bay window watching us with a phone pressed to her ear, waving.

Jake follows where my eyes are tracking and lifts a hand to wave. "She's also intense, your mom. I see where Travis gets it from, but she's really nice."

"She's one of my clients right now." Lifting a shoulder in the air, I sigh. "I got my first big break thanks to my mommy."

"You have to start somewhere. She seems like a busy woman. At dinner last night, she mentioned like, eight different clubs and committees she's a part of. What does she have you cater?"

"A few months ago, my mom hosted a fundraiser for a local food bank. All the money goes toward meals and grocery items for families in the area who are having it rough."

"That's a great cause, and one I heard about last night, too," he says with a chuckle.

"That's my mom. For this particular fundraiser, she'd talked a local French chef into doing a private meal for eight people as one of the auction items. Sadly, the chef had to pull out a few weeks ago due to a family emergency back in France. She was stuck, but Dad suggested I step in." Laughing softly, I shake my head at the memory. "She didn't like the idea at first, but I made a case for myself. I was sure I could do it, until she said yes. Then every doubt I've ever had about myself seemed to appear in front of me. It doesn't help that she likes to remind me that her reputation is intertwined with mine."

Another flicker of movement from the house pulls my attention. We both watch as the curtains sway closed and Mom disappears from our view. It makes me a little twitchy. I start looking in my rearview mirror and out the windows, which Jake picks up on pretty quickly.

"What are you doing?"

"She's like a shark. When I can't see her, I know she's in the water." Turning around in my seat, I look at the road behind us and grab my heart. I don't think as I reach out and put my hand on Jake's forearm—his very large, hard, and impressive forearm—and grip it to get his attention. "Look! I told you. She's at the mailbox now."

Jake swivels in his seat, his eyes widening, but he doesn't move his arm from underneath my hand. "How did she do that?"

"Secret tunnel? I don't know. The woman has weird powers. You saw Mandy cave when I mentioned her name at the rink. No one crosses Mad Dog."

"Mad Dog?"

"It's the name Travis and I gave her after a freak-out she had at a parent and teacher association event at our high school. She wasn't happy with how one of the teachers was treating students, and she stood up and had her say. It was like she came alive that night. I really don't remember her ever being so vocal about things in our community until then. She gave a speech that had the same fervor as a televangelist. Her eyes were wild, her gestures were exaggerated. It was like she mistook her moment to speak as her time in the spotlight, because she was into it." Do I giggle at the memory? You bet I do. "It was the night Mad Dog came out of her shell and hasn't looked back."

"Okay." Keeping his eyes on her as she walks up to my car, he nods his head. "I can see it."

"Be careful. She'll have you volunteer for something before you know what's happening."

Jake laughs but keeps an eye trained on my mom. "I'm

happy to donate some items if she needs them for a fundraiser."

I'm surprised when she simply taps on the hood of the car and then keeps on going back to the house, not even pausing to ask questions. Or to ask me how the menu is coming. Or anything.

Jake swings his head back to face me. "So you're in charge of a meal for your type-A mother. What does that look like?"

"Truffles."

"Like chocolate truffles? Does she know it's a meal of all sugar?"

"No, not that kind of truffles. Although I am serving some of the sweet truffles you're thinking of for dessert." I can feel my nerd hat coming out because this is a subject I like talking about. Food. "I'm using local savory truffles. It's the umami I'm theming the night around. I've got some friends who live near here and they have a truffle farm. They wanted some promotion for it, so they agreed to help sponsor the night and donate some truffles."

"You know, I've been out to eat at a few nice restaurants and I don't think I've ever gone for the truffle anything."

"Not even truffle fries?" I ask, my jaw going slack. "Come on, even the local bar serves those."

He looks at me woefully as he shrugs. "Nope. Never tried 'em."

"You need to fix that, and quickly." As I turn to meet his gaze, something shifts between us. It's a subtle, almost imperceptible change, but I can feel it nonetheless.

I can only speak for myself, but I'm feeling a mix of curiosity and anticipation, a quiet acknowledgment of some kind of connection. There's a quiet exchange between us, a silent conversation unfolding in the space between our gazes. It's as if we're testing the waters, exploring the unspoken possibilities that lie between us.

I could also be absolutely insane, but part of me is feeling a tug, deep in the very center of my core.

"Jake!"

The sound of someone calling his name makes our heads swivel in the direction of the house, where my mother is standing and waving at us. She points to Jake and holds up the home phone, an archaic thing to have in some circles, I know, but we do still have a landline here at the Richards property.

"You've got a phone call, dear," she yells out.

"I feel like we've been out on a date and are getting caught making out." Just him saying the words "making out" is enough to send a wild thrill of anticipation right through me.

Gripping the steering wheel, I smile and nod. "Yeah. Right? Making out." As soon as the words come out of my mouth, I want to shove them back in. What. A. Nerd.

"See ya later, Riley. Thanks for the ride." He opens the door and climbs out, the car suddenly emptier without his bulk next to me.

I watch as he sidles up the front path to the door, turning to wave as he goes inside, and I try hard to ignore the patter of my traitorous heart.

Walking up the steps to my little apartment in town, the song "Independent Women" by Destiny's Child always goes through my head. I love this place because I found it. I had a friend and realtor helping me look for places at the time, but this one I found on my own. I walked by the day that the landlord put a "for rent" sign in the front window.

The building used to be a three-story townhome but had been broken down into three separate apartments over the years. I live on the second floor, right above a couple who are a little bit...how do I put it politely? Let's just say they're two bricks shy of a load on a good day. The apartment above me is also occupied, but it's my landlord's super cool aunt, Frannie. She has owned it forever and doesn't live here full time. She saves it for trips she makes to Sweetkiss Creek. Like this week. I ran into her the other day at the market, so I know she's here.

Trudging up the steps to my place, the smell of soft florals hits my senses and I'm greeted by a huge bouquet of flowers sitting in front of my door. Roses, lilies, and tulips are piled into a giant glass vase, with fern and eucalyptus tucked in as well.

I get the door open, bending down to gather the arrangement in my arms before I go inside and kick the door closed behind me. Placing the bouquet on my kitchen table, I pluck out the card only to feel a little sick to my stomach when I read the note.

"If I have to send you more of these, I will. I'm sorry. I miss you, Riley. XO XO, Todd." Sighing, I lean against my desk and look down at the aquarium that houses my main man, and keeper of all my secrets by default, Brad Pitt the turtle.

I hold up the card to show him. "He keeps trying, but I'm just not that into him."

Brad turns his head in my direction; I know he's listening to me. He may also be sunning himself on a rock, but he's listening.

Shuddering, I head into the kitchen and pull out the ingredients I need to try out one of my appetizers for the bachelor auction. Potato flan with a truffle cream.

As I get the water boiling on the stove and start peeling potatoes, I can't help but let my thoughts drift back to when I dated Todd. Travis had warned me not to, but I had to play with fire. I let him sweep me off my feet. It started small, with a coffee date after we met at a game. I'd gone with Travis to watch some new clients of his play, and Todd was on the team.

He wasn't the Todd Taylor that people know now. These days, he's a hockey superstar who is known for being difficult to work with. I can say I saw it coming.

I turn on the oven and pull my premade truffle cream out of the fridge. I grab the molds I need and get everything organized before putting it in the oven. I've got fifty minutes.

While I wait, I run through the shower and try not to entertain the ickiness I feel inside that comes from having dated someone like Todd. Some women would like the fact that this guy was trying to get back in their good graces. It's the second time in the past month he's sent flowers. But I know the player, *and* the game.

I also know that humiliation is not my color.

My timer dings, letting me know that the appetizers are ready to try. I made way too many, but as long as at least one of them tastes good, I'll feel like I've got a solid handle on this dish.

As I open the oven door, I hear the front door to the apartment upstairs slam shut. Frannie must be home. Eyeing the flowers and the extra potato flan in front of me, I know exactly where this stuff can go.

A few minutes later, Frannie opens her door to my knock with a surprised look on her face as I hand her the bouquet.

"Again?" she asks with a wry smile. "Is that jerk head still trying to apologize?"

"You know it," I respond, waiting for her to put the flowers down before I hand her the plate. "I'm trying this dish —an appetizer—potato flan with a truffle cream. Have some and let me know what you think."

"You're the best neighbor ever. Thank you, dear." Frannie throws a thumb over her shoulder at a jersey that's still thrown across the back of her dining room chair. "I still need to pass on that jersey to my grandson. He's going to love it. I'm saving it for his birthday."

I eye the familiar fabric. It's Todd's jersey that I wore to a few games of his before the lies came out. "Shame it's Todd's..."

"I'm going to encourage him to sell it on eBay, don't you worry," she jokes as she squeezes my arm. "Or, maybe instead of giving it to him, I should use it for the Big Brothers Big Sisters program."

"Are you working on that fundraiser with my mom?"

"I sure am." Frannie floats across the foyer and places the bouquet on her dining room table. "Not sure why, but we have fewer adults in the area signing up than we've had in the past. It's discouraging, and we need more people."

Nodding my head, I cross my arms. "Do you think a fundraiser is going to do the trick?"

"I'm not convinced. I think we need a draw card, something bigger than a night of education, and silent auction items like gift cards to a coffee shop and the like, no offense to any cafe owners. It's just that it's a little boring, but don't you dare tell your mother I said that."

"Not a problem," I say with a giggle, still standing in her doorway. "But I think you're right. Any thoughts or ideas for a new way to recruit?"

"Not yet, but I'm brainstorming," Frannie says. "I feel like we need to get some people in who can speak to what the program is about and how they helped them."

"Like past little brothers and sisters who are now older and maybe paying it forward?"

"Yes, or ones who have gone on to great things. Like the Porter boys."

"Oh, that is true!" My head nods automatically. "I always forget those two grew up without a dad."

"Yep. Their mom is amazing. She's mentioned to me in the past that the Big Brothers Big Sisters program helped her and them at a time when she was at her wit's end."

The Porter brothers are not only my truffle supplier, but they're also a little bit famous for these parts. Both boys were stars of our football team in high school and have gone on to play for opposing NFL teams. They're absolute dreamboats who Travis and I grew up with. Levi and Austin are hilarious, a trait that is showcased on their weekly podcast they host together.

"You know, I'm going to see them this week to pick up some truffles. Do you want me to feel them out for you?"

Frannie's eyes light up. "Would you? That would be amazing. They are the kind of draw that I think could get more adults to sign up once they hear their story."

"I'm happy to see what they say." I take a step back and toss a hand in the air. "I'll let you know what happens."

We say goodbye and I head back to my place, closing the door behind me. The slight movement sends the scent of something like clean sheets and sandalwood to my senses, and a snap of excitement makes me sigh.

It smells like Jake.

SEVEN
Jake

Sweetkiss Creek is quiet this morning. I like sneaking in a run as often as I can, but I love doing it first thing in the day, and if I can do it when the rest of the world is either just waking up or maybe slowly realizing it's time to get up, even better.

Riley's dad had to leave to open the cafe early this morning, so I hitched a ride and had him drop me off at a campground just outside of town so I could make my way in. He's a man of many facets, and cars. Today, he came in his Prius, but I can't lie I was hoping he'd fire up the '63 Mustang. Maybe another day.

Starting my day jogging beside a lake sounded like something I could use right now to clear my head. There was one thing, or one person, who keeps hanging out rent-free in my thoughts, and if I'm honest with myself, I don't mind it. Not one bit.

From the moment she jumped into the back of my car and scared the crap outta me, I've been pretty intrigued by this woman. Travis has told me about his little sister, who his dad adores but apparently makes her mom crazy. I have friends with kids who would attest to the fact that it's a mother-and-daughter thing. I wonder what Riley would say it was?

The morning air has a chill, but there's warmth in the sunshine today. I never thought that beginning this year with my new team I'd be ending it trying to go back to my old one, and pretty much in the doghouse with a handful of people I respect with all of my heart. I'd made the jump from the River City Renegades to be seen—I had a chance to get on a team with several other players who it's been rumored are on their way to the NHL.

When I was asked to join them, I saw an opportunity. In my mind, I could get on that team and not only make a bigger name for myself there, but as other players climbed out of AHL status and moved up to the next league, I wanted to at least replace them if I wasn't going with them. Everything I heard about the team sounded like it would be a good move. One I could make smoothly and easily, a path with the least resistance.

Only it wasn't. Concentrating on my feet as they land on the ground, crunching the rock on the gravel path, I'm reminded of the not-so-welcome welcome I was given when I arrived. I was barely acknowledged, not that I needed to always be, but I was new. You would think that being a team, the dynamics would be different. Well, they were, but it was that they were different from the team I had chosen to leave. The captain of the team, known in the press for being a bit of a narcissistic butthole but also loved because he's a really amazing player (things I'll never understand about the human psyche), tried to fight me on the ice that first day.

I'm not the kind of guy who stands down from anything, but I do try to stay away from trouble. My dad taught me better than that. I'm also big, so why get into a fight with anyone? But when you've got someone your size or even bigger slamming into you on purpose over and over, and in your first practice, you begin to think it's more than a simple hazing.

The team I'd come from? The best. The Renegades are like, the most supportive group ever. Our coach, a family man who always had his kids around helping out. The players made sure that if anyone came into our house and was new to the team, no matter if they were on the ice with us, worked in the arena, or in the offices, they felt like family. It was a family, a great big wonderful one that stuck together, even hanging out on holidays, and I had to go and split it up.

I slow down to check my time only to find a news alert has popped up on my phone. Not to sound narcissistic myself, but due to this reporter who's trying to tear me down, I'd set up an alert on my name. And it looks like she's at it again.

"Jake December's career in limbo." I take a calming breath in through my nose and breathe it all out through my mouth slowly, taking a second to bend over and touch my toes, hanging there limp and swaying. "Why, Greta. Why are you doing this to me?"

"Ummm," a voice says slowly, laughing, "are you aware there's no one named Greta around?"

Standing up straight, my heart slams in my chest when I look into the eyes of a giggling Riley. She's got her hair pulled back into a bun at the base of her neck and is wearing a trucker hat with the Renegades logo on it. I don't think she has a trace of makeup on, yet she's glowing, which can be a feat at this time of morning for anyone. Superheroes included.

To put it in normal dude speak, she looks hot. I'd go so far as to say she's on fire. And it's not even eight in the morning.

"Hey," I manage, trying to hide the nervous stutter that threatens. It's an old anxiety trait I've had to work on over the years.

Riley eyes me with a mischievous grin. "So, Greta. Is she someone worth noting?"

"No." I hold up a hand to stop her from saying anything more, and her eyes widen. "Sorry, I think I said that with a little more aggression than I meant to."

"Hey. No problem here." Riley holds up a hand, waving it in the air as if she's wiping the moment away. "I shouldn't have been nosy."

We're standing at the edge of Lake Lorelei in a small park with a promenade that links to the main street in town. The edges of the small park are lined with garden beds bursting with colorful flowers like phlox, tulips, irises, and daffodils. A few park benches and picnic tables are scattered about, partly filled by people sipping on their coffees and playing games of chess or checkers.

There's also an old fountain in the middle of the green space, right behind Riley, and on the other side of that is a coffee cart that's set up and open for the morning crowd. The ambient noise of water as it rolls onto the lakeshore is calming.

Inclining my head toward the cart, I lock my eyes with hers. "Were you doing another delivery?"

"Oh, you bet I was." She throws a thumb over her shoulder to the cart. "Three days a week I'm down here, dropping off their order. I usually go for a run afterward."

"Ah." I feel like I'm being cued to something, so I step back. "Don't let me keep you."

"Actually," she says as she looks around, "I woke up on the back foot this morning. Is that even a saying?"

"It is, but I think it's meant that you'd be defensive. Like, in a less than advantageous position compared to someone you're opposing." When I see the look on her face, I crack a smile. "I'm a bit of a nerd. When I was in college, I took a class in linguistics and did a study on idioms."

I can tell she's biting back her laughter. Her lips aren't moving, but her eyes give it away.

"That's unexpected."

"I pride myself on being full of surprises."

"I'm surprised to have run into you again so soon," she quips. "So. Is Greta also a surprise?"

Rolling my eyes, I slip my body into a standing hamstring stretch. "Greta is someone I once kinda dated. Things ended, I thought amicably, but apparently she doesn't feel the same way."

She cocks her head to the side. "And she's making your life hard right now?"

"She's a sports reporter who has the power of the internet and social media behind her."

"Ahhh. So she's enjoying the fact you're a man without a team right now and seen as a wild card?"

"That's putting it lightly, but yeah. She's enjoying it because it gets her headlines."

"And you didn't do anything to make her mad when you broke up?"

"I thought I handled it all the best way I could. I took her out for dinner..."

Riley's face scrunches. "Ohhhh. Please don't tell me you did it in public."

"I mean, the conversation leaned that way at dinner, so I went with it."

"You took her out to eat, and without warning you broke things off in a public setting so she had to hold it all in—if she held it all in, that is—until you left and were somewhere more private to talk, then?"

"I mean..." I'm finding it somewhat comical that I'm having to explain this right now. "I was coming from practice and she was coming from work, so we met at the restaurant."

"You may be emotionally stunted." Riley's face is serious as she threads her arms tightly in front of her chest. "You didn't even drive her home after or offer to talk further, did you?"

"Well..." I search my brain for an answer, any kind that won't make me sound as much of a buffoon as it does now, but I've got nothing. In less than two minutes, this new-to-me woman has shown me the mirror and pointed out where I went wrong. "Yeah, no. I thought we were good when we left. I paid the bill and we hugged outside, and that was that."

"Oh, man. And she's a reporter?" Riley does a tsk tsk as she shakes her head. "I've been around my brother long enough to know that there's optics to consider in every part of what you do once you're playing at a certain level, Jake. But you went and dated a sports reporter and then you broke up with her in public? Ohhhh, poor you. She's gonna want revenge for sure."

"You're not helping," I mutter as I start to stretch my other leg. But she's got a point.

"Sorry. I'll drop it. No more Greta speak. We'll call her Voldemort, okay?"

This woman has dropped a Harry Potter reference and I'm here for it. "Deal."

Riley, whose arms had been crossed tightly in front of her, lets them drop to her side. Turning at the waist, she points behind her to the coffee cart. "Want to have a coffee with me? My treat."

I look at the cart, then back to Riley. I could say no. Go on my way, keep running, and then go to the rink to practice like I was planning. I could do that and then go back to thinking about my mistakes, the choices I've made, and where I'm at now and probably continue to beat myself up some more. I'll end up back at home, well, Riley's home in her old bedroom, holding my dog and wondering where I went wrong. So of course I'm going to say yes.

"Love to." I hold my hand out. "Lead the way."

As we approach the cart, the older man running it appears

in the window with a huge grin sweeping across his face, showing all of his teeth.

"Riley. You're still here?"

"Yes, Sam, and we need the things."

Sam laughs, loud and deep. The man looks like he's related to Santa Claus.

"How about my famous Moroccan mint lattes for both of you? I can also highly recommend these amazing croissants we have in stock this morning."

Riley nods. "Put 'em on my tab, Sam."

"You got it, Riley. Oh, and I'll make sure to get you or Frannie that gift voucher for her giveaway. It's nice what you're trying to do. That organization needs all the help it can get."

"Thanks, Sam, she'll appreciate it." Riley turns back to me, finding me staring at her quizzically. "What?"

"Giveaway?"

"My neighbor works with the local Big Brothers Big Sisters charity, and they need some help recruiting people. They're doing giveaways on social media and planning a fundraiser. She's been busy trying to figure out a way to get adults interested in taking part again."

"That's an important program." I nod with acknowledgment. Anyone who volunteers their time like that will always get my respect. I make a mental note to look into volunteering myself when, and if, I get back to River City.

Santa Sam is back, sliding our goods across the counter. Riley hands me my drink, taking hers and our bag of pastries, and I follow her over to the fountain.

"Here." She parks on its edge, patting the spot next to her.

Planting myself beside her, I cast a glance at the tranquil fountain, its waters still as it's yet to be turned on for the day. At the bottom of its pool lies what could be hundreds of dollars in change.

I nod toward the fountain. "Do people come here and make wishes?"

Riley nods. "It's a thing, you know. If you're in town, you bring some coins and toss 'em in and make a wish." She reaches into her bag, pulling out her wallet. Unzipping its pouch, she grabs out a penny for each of us.

"Here." She hands me one as she closes her eyes and tosses hers in. Snapping her eyes open, she looks at me, then to the penny in my hand. "Your turn. Make a wish."

"Can you tell me what you wished for?" When I see the look in her eyes, I hold my hands up in mock surrender. "I need ideas."

"Get your own wish." She laughs.

Closing my eyes, I think hard for a second. What do I want to wish for? World peace is too broad and feels like a huge ask, but it's up there along with finding a home team again, or rather, having my old one accept me back. But then there's also the wish I have to be more settled. The recent urge I've had to feel grounded. Invested. Committed.

"Come on," Riley whispers, nudging my knee. "Your coffee is gonna get cold."

I let go of the penny, tossing it in the air as I say a silent prayer and let my wish go with it.

When I open my eyes, I find Riley staring at me intensely.

"So, wanna tell me what it was?"

"Get your own wish," I retort, making the gleam in her eyes burn brighter.

"Good answer," she says as she hands me one of the croissants from the little brown bakery bag she's clutching. "Nothing like starting the morning like a sugar champion."

"Pretty sure this is not on my in-season diet." I take the croissant she's handed to me and smell it. "Seriously. Cinnamon and chocolate? That's the best flavor combo ever."

"Right? I love the combo." She takes a bite, and my eyes

make their way to her lips where a tiny flake of pastry has parked itself on the outer corner.

I point to my face, mimicking the spot where her piece of pastry lies. "You've got something."

"I do?" Her hand flies to her mouth as she wipes everywhere except the spot where the pastry sits. "Did I get it?"

"Not quite." Shaking my head, and smiling because I can't help it, I point to my face and try again. "Here."

She lifts her hand and again wipes all around her cheeks, chin, and lips, but somehow the world's most bonded piece of croissant flake holds its location. "I got it that time, surely."

I know she's looking at me, but I'm busy looking at the spot on her lips that's in question. Full, pink lips that are perfect, like a Cupid's bow. Smooth, beautiful lips that I'm now fighting the urge to lean over and kiss.

As soon as the thought hits me, a cold blast of ice hits my system. *This is Travis's little sister,* my head screams. *But she's also a gorgeous woman,* my heart yells back.

Calming myself, and both the angel and the devil sitting on my shoulder right now telling me to do all the things, I hold my hand up, close to her face.

"May I?"

Sparkling sea-green eyes hold mine, crinkling at the corners as she smiles. "Please."

I lift my hand closer, reaching out with my thumb to brush it away. It falls off almost immediately, floating away and down to the ground. But I take my time and lightly rub my thumb across her lip as I scoot in closer to her. A heady scent of gardenia hits my senses. Is it wrong that I want this one moment to last for a very long time? And I'll eke it out more than I have to if I can. Trust me.

The sound of water splashing and tumbling around us fills the air as the fountain comes to life for the day. A splash of cold water sprays across the side of my face, making my jaw go slack. Startled, Riley jumps to her feet, throwing her head back and laughing when she realizes what's happening.

"That freaked me out!" she declares as she sits back down, angling her body so we're still close. She smacks her lips together and closes her eyes, and my heart does a triple beat. I swear she's reading my mind. Could she tell I was daydreaming about kissing her?

"So?" she finally says.

"Yes?" I respond, my voice breathy. I know. I'm starting to be a little over the top, but I'm feeling vulnerable these days.

Her eyes snap back open. "Did you get the food off my face?"

It's my turn to chew back a grin, which I do as I also slide a few inches back. I need to undo this electrical charge that's flowing through my body and fast.

"Yes, it's gone." I pick up the croissant from my lap and take a big bite, letting the flakes fall everywhere, all down the front of me and onto my lap. "How about me? Did I drop anything?"

"You're an actual hot mess." Giggling, she wipes at my chest and stomach, stopping for a moment as she does. It can't be a coincidence, but I swear I felt her hand flex as she stroked my abs. My eyes skip to hers and I see her jaw clench as she takes a tight breath. She pulls her hand away like she's just touched a hot stovetop and jumps to her feet.

"I have a feeling," she says, clearing her throat as she looks at her watch. "Yep, I need to get going. I have an appointment this morning."

"You're not trying to get away from me and my problems?" I tease, not wanting the morning time with Riley to end.

"I need to see a man about some truffles," she says with a wink. "Actually mens, I need to see two mens about some truffles."

"Mens? Like two men?"

"So I said mens, so what?" She's smiling this smile that's new to me in this conversation. This one is light and playful, and I can't help but notice that she wrinkles her nose when she leans forward. "My friends have a farm outside of town and I get my truffles from them. I need to drive out and pick up my order for the private dinner."

"Do you need company?"

Riley eyes me. "Don't you need to practice or something?"

I shrug. "I can do it later. The rink is open until ten tonight, so there's plenty of time."

"Okay, December." She runs her eyes across me, taking in my outfit. "I take it you need to change and shower before we go?"

"If you don't mind."

"Not at all. I have some calls I need to make and can do that from anywhere." She pulls her keys out and shakes them in the air as she tosses our trash away and grabs her coffee cup. "Let's go."

Walking side by side with Riley to her car, there's a thrill inside of me. I want to be closer to her, to get to know her more. I can't even explain what the pull is to her, I only know I had it the moment I laid eyes on her. Now that I'm getting to know her, there's more going on.

But that doesn't change the fact that she's still my best friend's little sister.

EIGHT
Riley

After a quick pit stop for Jake to shower and change, we're on the road. I'd even managed to avoid running into my mother, who had texted me earlier in the morning asking if she could suggest a dish to serve for the dinner while also asking if I was dating anyone new. It's a question she likes to ask me every few months, but for some reason leaves Travis alone. Shouldn't the eldest sibling be the one to be quizzed on that kind of thing? I have an unholy fear that she'll do something insane like try to set me up with someone. I love this woman dearly, but her inserting herself into my love life is the last thing I need.

Beside me, in the passenger seat, Jake looks around. He opens the glove box and pulls out a box of tissues and the leftovers from a candy bar, plus another odd-looking white plastic contraption no bigger than a small votive that he holds in the air.

"What's this?" he asks.

"Why are you looking at my things?" My laugh is nervous because I can't remember what all I have in here. I wouldn't be surprised if a bra fell out onto his feet, I've been that busy lately.

"You can learn a lot about someone when you get into their car." He holds up the plastic item again. "So, any thoughts?"

I take it from his hand and, removing my eyes from the road for a second, glance at it quickly. Still unsure, I hold it to my nose and take a sniff.

"What are you doing?"

"Smelling it, duh," I say, handing it back to him. "It smells like watermelon, which means it's the remnants of a candy ring. You know, the kind that looks like a giant diamond, but it's candy?"

"I know what you're talking about." He chortles. "You kept the base?"

"Not on purpose. I was probably cleaning the car quickly and tossed it in the glove box. Or it's a reminder for me to order some. I can never find them and I love them."

"Good for a road trip," he acknowledges, putting the tiny ring remnants, and the other contents he'd pulled out, back in their place.

The Porter Family Farm is about thirty minutes outside of town. I love the drive to their place and always have. My favorite part is when we get out of Sweetkiss Creek proper and the scenery begins to shift around us. Narrow roads wind their way through rolling hills adorned with patches of vibrant greenery and splashes of wildflowers, painting a picturesque scene that feels like it's been plucked straight from a postcard.

As you go further into the countryside, the landscape gradually transforms, giving way to rugged mountains that loom majestically in the distance. Their peaks are cloaked in a soft haze, lending an air of nostalgia and grandeur to the surrounding landscape.

The road twists and turns, offering breathtaking views at

every bend we go around. To one side, you can catch glimpses of babbling brooks and cascading waterfalls, their soothing sounds blending harmoniously with the hum of the engine. To the other, towering trees stretch toward the sky, their leaves rustling gently in the mountain breeze.

Jake turns up the volume on the radio while we ascend higher into the mountains. Without even rolling the window down, I can tell that the air has grown crisper and cooler, and when I crack my window, I'm met with the heady scent of pine and earth. The sunlight filters through the dense canopy above, dappling the road with patches of golden warmth.

"I forget how stunning it can be around here," Jake murmurs from his seat. He's angled himself so he's facing me. "River City isn't a giant city, but it's not full of trees and all the green space that Sweetkiss Creek has."

"They have a park. It's beautiful. I've been there several times over the years for events with my family, most recently for the River City Fair, which is a whole amazing day out in and of itself. Have you been?"

"No," Jake responds, laughter in his voice. "But I guess if it's happening the next time I'm in town, I'll have to make sure I go."

"One hundred percent. It's the best. Fresh squeezed lemonade, funnel cakes, prizes for the biggest vegetables, I think they had a lumberjack competition last year...and those are just the highlights."

"Sold."

There's an ease and cadence to our conversation that I can't deny. There's also an insane magnetic pull that I'm having to this man whenever he's near me, much like this morning. Seeing him across the park area by the lakefront, standing on the other side of the fountain, my heart had slammed in my chest. Which is just not like me. I even repeated in my head, *He's a hockey player, do not go there. He is a hockey player, do NOT go there,* over and over as I walked over to him. It didn't help.

Sneaking a peek at him out of my peripheral vision, I can just make out the strong line of his jaw. He hasn't shaved for a few days, so the clean, fresh-faced player I met a few days ago is gone; this guy looks like he could morph into a rugged mountain man. Just the thought of seeing him in a flannel shirt gives my skin a case of the goosebumps that any doctor would question.

Gripping the wheel, I concentrate on the road. I need to get us there in one piece.

A high-pitched ring pierces the air of my car, the dashboard showing that I'm receiving a call. Jake points to the screen.

"Ummm, so Dad's Wife is calling?"

Yes, she's on my phone as Dad's Wife today. Two days ago, she was The Monster, and a week before that, she was Mouth of the South after she told her bridge club I was undateable in her opinion. The only reason I found out she said this was because one of Georgie's customers came in and saw me working, and feeling bad for me, bought me a self-help book and a book about makeovers, leaving them for me at the counter as a gift. Georgie still laughs about it while I threaten to make her eat the books.

Pressing the button on my steering wheel, I put a fake smile on when I answer. "Hello, Mother."

"Riley Richards, is that menu going to be ready for me to do a tasting before you serve it? You know I want to have at least an idea of how it's going to be."

She's abrupt and her tone is sharp. A quick glance at Jake, and I can see this is not the side of my mother he's been used to seeing while he's been here. My mother is intense, but she's a perfectionist, too. She's also got this thing about looking absolutely perfect to the outside world.

I liken it to this drawer we have at the back of the kitchen, near the back door, and it's the bottom one. You see, every other drawer in our kitchen is organized—drawer liners, containers, rack organizers for our pots, even the spices are labeled and all put away in beautiful glass jars.

But this one drawer is the catch-all. It has takeout menus, spools of thread, a ball of twine, scissors, slips of paper, tools like a small hammer and a screwdriver, and also tiny packets of plant food, like the kind that comes with floral bouquets. There are old photos, including some that go as far back as elementary school, of Travis and me.

Whenever I open that drawer, it screams. It's loud. It doesn't fit in the room, yet it does. Because it's like my mother. Surrounded by so many pretty and perfect things on the outside, she's the kind of woman who when asked how she is plasters on her best beauty-queen smile and purrs, "Everything's fine. I'm fine. We're fine! Things are good." And she'll say this even if we're standing in the middle of a hurricane with snow falling around us as aliens are landing.

I take great pleasure in calling this drawer the "everything's fine" drawer.

"I'm in the car now headed out to the Porter farm for supplies, Mom. I'm planning on doing a practice run tomorrow night."

"So you're coming here, to the house?" she asks, her tone clipped and a little distracted. Pretty much sums up my time with her when I was a teen.

I glance at Jake, whose brow is furrowed as he listens, and he mouths the word sorry. "I wasn't going to, but I'm happy to do that if it makes you feel better. I've been planning this truffle chicken..."

"Sounds good," she interjects, cutting me off. That's her. She's heard what she needs to hear from me and now she's done. "I'll see you here tomorrow night, then."

"Do I get to try some, too?" Jake asks as I use my hand to make a karate chop motion at him, slicing it through the air as if I can stop her from hearing that he's with me.

"You didn't tell me you had someone with you." My mother's voice suddenly shifts and changes. Her tone is syrupy sweet, kinder, and she's taken it up an octave. Here's the woman everyone else gets to see. "I think that must be Jake I hear?"

I shoot him a look as he shrugs. "It is. Riley kindly offered to show me around, so I'm tagging along to see this farm today."

"Don't forget to get to the rink and do your drills." She chuckles. When did she get so savvy in hockey-speak? Not that drills are hockey-speak, but come on. "Travis will kill us if we don't take care of you and keep you on schedule. You've got a reputation to uphold."

Biting my lip, I shake my head and try not to laugh. Of course, she'd round it back to reputation. Jake squirms in his seat, his shoulders shaking.

"Yes, ma'am, you're right. I'll make sure to practice once we're done."

"Good." She's quiet, and I can almost hear the gears turning in that head of hers. "Well, I guess I'll talk to you later, Riley. Drive safe and have fun, you two."

And the line goes silent. Jake opens his mouth to speak, but I hold up a hand to stop him, taking that moment to press "phone off" on my screen.

"Sorry, I just wanted to make sure we were properly disconnected before we spoke," I say with a laugh. "And now, you've met the real side of my mother."

"Does she always talk to you like that?"

Lifting a shoulder, I let it drop as I slow the car down. "Not all the time."

"She's not like that with Travis. And she definitely doesn't act that way when I'm around her."

Hitting my blinker, I turn onto the old country road that will take us to the Porter's. "And she won't. I think it's just me who she gets a little crazy with. My dad thinks she just wants the best for me, but I feel like there's some disappointment laced with competition, if that makes sense? Like she wanted me to follow in her footsteps, but because I'm a little more independent than that and I do things my way, she wants to go tit for tat sometimes."

Jake's quiet, but I can see him nodding his head out of the corner of my eye. "Parents are tricky, aren't they?"

"Do you have something going on with your parents, too?"

He shakes his head. "My mother died when I was younger, and my dad has always worked hard to be here for me. Had two jobs to keep up on the bills and pay for my hockey lessons. But in working so hard, he built a wall of anxiety that has shown up as hoarding. He's been in and out of therapy over the past two years for it."

"Oh, wow," I manage to say, my heart aching just hearing this. "I'm so sorry about that. How is he now?"

"He's good, getting better each day. But he's the one I do this for." Jake gets quiet, and when I look out of the corner of my eye, I see he's gazing out the window, watching the world go by. "I promised myself I'd be the one to take care of him, so now it's my turn. I don't want him to ever want for anything. I want him to feel as safe as he made me feel at a time when we were at our most vulnerable."

I stay quiet as he continues. "I think it's why I respect and also appreciate your brother so much. He gets me, and he knows why I show up to the rink every day, why I want to do well at hockey. If I do well, I get paid doing what I love. And that means the people I love are taken care of."

Jake stops talking abruptly before turning his body fully toward the passenger window. Getting the feeling he needs a minute to breathe, I take my cue and focus on the road ahead. He hasn't said a lot, but what he has shared is big. Heavy. He's carrying a load of his own, and if he isn't careful, he could buckle under the pressure. I don't want to be the one to trip him up. In fact, the more I get to know him, the more I want to help him.

Sighing, I turn up the volume on the radio and sit back, thinking about Jake's father, going through hoarding as a result of his anxiety after the love of his life passed away. But the lengths he went to for his son? Amazing.

I look at Jake; he's turned back around and facing the right way, his eyes closed. Within a matter of minutes, I'm tapping his leg and pointing to a driveaway ahead of us.

"We're here," I say as I hit the brakes and maneuver the car up the long entrance to the Porter Farm. Not going to lie, though. I'd like to keep on driving so we can keep on talking, because there's more to this hulk of a man than meets the eye.

NINE

Riley

"When I was a little girl, we came out here every weekend to see the Porters." Getting out of the car, I look around at the familiar turf and can't help but grin. I've had some of my best summer weekends at this place.

I point to a large orchard toward the back of the property, just behind a large barn. "That's the truffle orchard. Mary, she's the matron of the family, specializes in growing them here. She started farming truffles about ten years ago. Someone my dad knows introduced her to the idea of planting loblolly pine seedlings, with inoculations of truffles, and before you knew it they were in business and became one of the first white truffle farms in North Carolina."

Jake stands with his hands in his pockets looking around beside me. He nods his head toward the open barn door. There's a country song spilling out and someone is singing off-key. "Is that where your friends are?"

"That wounded animal is probably Levi." I flick a hand over my shoulder and head toward the building. "Follow me."

Swinging the barn door open to its full potential, a wave of excitement washes over me. The converted space is one of my favorite things about the farm.

The rustic charm of the barn has been preserved, with exposed wooden beams overhead and the faint scent of hay lingering in the air. But instead of housing livestock, it's been transformed into a vibrant workspace that exudes creativity and fun.

Colorful bean bag chairs are scattered throughout the open floor plan, inviting impromptu brainstorming sessions and casual meetings. Pops of bright hues adorn the walls, injecting energy and personality into the space.

One corner of the barn has been converted into a cozy lounge area, complete with plush couches and oversized floor pillows. It's the perfect relaxed setting to kick back and unwind after a long day of work.

In another corner, beside a pile of hay that one of the boys no doubt brought inside to make the other crazy, a ping-pong table takes center stage and adds a playful energy to the already brilliant atmosphere.

The barn's large windows flood the space with natural light, creating a warm and inviting ambiance that inspires creativity and productivity. Plants hang from the rafters, adding a touch of greenery and infusing the space with life.

"Riley!" Levi sings out as he leaps up from his desk. He crosses the barn in a few giant steps and pulls me into his arms. Laughing, I let him spin me around until we're right dizzy. He drops me into a giggling heap beside him as he hugs me close. "I feel like I've not seen you in years. How are you?"

"Good, busy. Moved out, quit the cafe, and started my own business." I cross my arms in front of my chest. "That about sums it up. You?"

"Awesome, and tired. Played well this year—we made it to

the quarter-finals, but now I'm on a break until practice starts for the season again." Levi is the quarterback for one of the NFL's top teams. We thought we had a Super Bowl championship in the bag this year, but the team was plagued by injuries, including Levi's. He holds up his right hand. "This baby is still healing, but we're getting there."

His eyes rock to Jake, who stands behind me still, quiet. Levi's eyes widen with surprise as he steps forward and holds out his hand. "You're Jake December. Dude!" He looks up at the loft and catches his brother's eyes. "Man, it's Jake freaking December! He's here in our barn!"

Glancing at Jake, I can tell he's as surprised as I am. But we don't have a chance to let it sink in because one whoop hello later, and Austin actually swings down from the loft above us on a rope, dropping into a small pile of hay near us.

Honestly, I think they're showing off now. I've never seen these two act like this.

"Jake? Man, we've been watching your games since you started with the Renegades, then went to the Blades," Austin says as he grabs his hand and pumps it. He then reaches out and pulls me into a quick hug. "What are you doing here with Riley?"

"It's Travis, isn't it?" Levi nods his head knowingly. "Travis is your agent, right?"

Levi is, in a weird way, all-knowing. He was always the softer one of these two. He's the guy who prefers to sneak into a documentary film over the next big action drama that's hitting the big screen, or he'll get tickets to the ballet or a Broadway show instead of going to see a concert. I've spent many nights in our early twenties accompanying him to art gallery openings so he had a date. A friendly date, that's all we were and are. These two are like bonus big brothers I never asked for but ended up with anyway.

"He is," Jake acknowledges as he reaches out and squeezes my arm. "But today, I'm in Riley's capable hands. She said she was coming out to a working truffle farm, so I tagged along. But you guys, you're *the* Porter brothers?"

Levi chuckles. "According to our mother, yes."

"I'm a fan. Of both of yours. On the field and on your podcast."

Of course these guys are getting on like nobody's business. Me? I'm still staring at Jake's hand on my arm. I don't have any time to overthink his touch before four dogs come flying into the barn, barking and playing, tumbling around in a small pack. Austin inclines his head in their direction. "Those are our dogs we use for finding the truffles."

"You use dogs?" Jake asks.

"Come up here to the loft and let me show you the farm. You get a great view from the window up there." He looks at me and winks. "As long as Riley doesn't mind that I'm stealing her date?"

"Like I'd bring a date here." I stick my tongue out. "It'll give me time to do business with the smarter brother, thank you very much." I turn to Jake with a serious look as I point to the rope. "Don't let him make you climb that to get up there. You'll kill yourself."

When Jake's eyes grow larger, Levi chuckles. "Ignore her. She likes to stir people up." He waves a hand to the stairs on the side of the barn. "Those will take you up safely."

He then turns to me. "Let's get your order sorted out. I just need you to sign your pickup form and you're set."

Movement from the barn door catches my attention. Looking over, there's a dog peeking at us from the other side of the door.

"Another truffle dog?" I ask Levi, following him to his desk.

"I wish." Levi glances up at the little guy, who is slowly

making his way into the barn, timidly but he's coming. "That's Becks. He's not up to snuff for what we need."

"Up to snuff?" I grab at my heart in faux shock. "That's just mean."

"The dogs we have are all truffle hunters, and he's not that into it. In fact, the only thing he's good at finding is dirty laundry."

"We all need something," I insist, not liking hearing that someone, in this case a four-legged someone, doesn't fit in. When I cast my eyes back in the direction where the dog had been hovering, I'm surprised to see he's made his way over so he's now sitting about a foot from me. He's black and white, a medium-sized border collie, with eyes that are each a different color: one is icy blue, the other a forest green. "He is cute, Levi. Are you guys spoiling him since he's not a working dog?"

Levi shakes his head, his expression downcast. "We can't keep him. Austin and I aren't here most of the year because of football, and due to time and resources, Mom can only handle four dogs. Becks was supposed to be the fourth dog, but after a two-month trial, it became evident he wasn't going to be what we needed, so Mom replaced him. She kept him around waiting for us to get back so we could decide what to do. I think she was hoping one of us would volunteer to keep him."

Sparkling eyes catch mine, and there's a tug at my heart as this dog slides to his belly and places his head on his front paws, watching me. But the sound of two rowdy men upstairs laughing breaks the serene moment.

"Well, those two get along," I say, my eyes scanning the loft. I flick them back to Levi, who is watching me with a grin spread across his smug face. "What?"

"You're bringing a hockey player out here? Of course we're going to get along, we love hockey."

"So, what's the deal?"

"It's you." Levi's eyes rock to the loft then back to me.

"And a hockey player. You told me you were done with these types."

"He's not anything more than one of Travis's friends and a client."

"Yeah, whatever," Levi murmurs. "I've got radar for this, I'm a guy. As soon as Austin hugged you, December made sure to grab your arm so we'd know..."

"So you'd know what?" I'm laughing now. "You're trying to stir me up now, aren't you?"

You know those moments when you can feel someone is watching you? I'm having one now, so I look back up at the loft not expecting to see anything, but I'm surprised when I find Jake looking down at me. He holds my gaze for a moment before he smiles. Austin calls his name out from behind and he disappears again, leaving me to slowly pull my attention back to Levi.

"See," he says, with something more than smugness dripping on each word. "He is watching you. I'm telling you..."

"Stop talking." I laugh as I lean forward and put my hands on his makeshift desk. "Hey, you know how you and Austin were in the Big Brothers Big Sisters program?"

Levi nods. "Best thing to happen to us. Don't know if we would have ended up in football if we hadn't been enrolled."

"That's what I thought. Look, my mom is trying to put together a fundraiser for the one in Sweetkiss Creek. Maybe you guys have some cool swag I can throw into the auction?"

"What are you thinking?"

I shrug. "I don't know. Jersey? Tickets to a game? A date?" The last suggestion is a joke, but Levi's eyebrows shoot up.

"A date?" He scratches his chin. "I'd like to offer Austin up for a date."

"Stop it," I say, tossing a piece of paper at his head. "Forget I said date and have a think about a jersey or tickets or something. Maybe a meet and greet with both of you? I'll supervise."

"I'll talk to Austin and see what we can do." Levi then levels his gaze at me. "But now, about that hockey player..."

"What?" Austin says from where he's descending the stairs. "What kind of drama are you filling in Riley's head now?"

Snapping the invoice from Levi's hand, I find a pen and scribble my name across it. "He's trying to get me to take Becks off your hands, that's what he's doing."

"Seriously?" Levi whispers as his eyes light up. I knew this was the change of subject I needed. But now, I've got one of my oldest and dearest friends thinking I want a dog. "If you took Becks, that would be awesome. Would you still bring him out so we could see him?"

"Well, there's Brad Pitt..."

"He's a turtle."

Jake's eyes light up. "You have a turtle?"

"He's my baby." I look back at Levi. "Seriously, I'm not even sure I can have a dog at my new place."

"Come on, trial basis?" He grins as he opens a desk drawer and pulls out a leash. "I'll throw in a leash for free."

"Only a leash?"

"How about the first month of dog food, a new dog bed, and his next round of shots." Levi throws his hands in the air. "Please, Riley? I honestly don't want to get rid of this dog, but if he goes with you, then I know he'll be safe. And happy."

"And he can see him again because he's a sucker," Austin says, tossing a handful of hay at his brother's head.

I look at Jake, who is busy trying not to laugh. "It's a responsibility I'm not sure I can..."

"Dogs are the best kind of responsibility," Jake interjects, looking at the Porter brothers. "Not trying to butt in, just advocating for Becks over there."

I feel like there's a giant spotlight on me. Shaking my head, I drag my eyes back to Levi. "Trial basis. Right?"

Levi's out of the chair before he answers. "Yes! I'll go get some of his things, and we'll get him and your truffles loaded up for you. Seriously, you're the best. I miss spending time with you, Riley. Everyone needs a friend like you." He scoops me into a big hug as he passes me.

"A friend who is also a giant sucker?" I tease, slapping at his back as he jogs away.

Austin laughs, shoving his hands deep in his pockets. "He's been planning on asking you to take Becks for the last few weeks, you know."

"Are you serious?" I half choke out. I throw my hands in the air. "And I told Jake you two were good guys."

"We are," Austin says with a wink before turning to Jake. "Hey, tell Travis I'll be in touch soon. I may be jumping to his ship."

Jake nods. "You may know him as a friend, but as an agent, he's the best. He'll do you right, I promise."

Austin waves as he jogs away, following Levi to get our order—and my new dog—in the car for us.

What am I thinking?

Spinning back around, I collide with Jake, who is suddenly standing oh-so-close to me, and fall smack into his arms. His presence sends a shiver of anticipation down my spine. All I can see when I look at him are his lips. Beautiful full lips.

What is wrong with me? This is not like me at all. AT ALL. I don't do this, I don't obsess randomly over men I've just met. It's bewildering to me, but that doesn't change the fact that we're still pressed against each other and neither one of us is budging.

"Hey," he murmurs, putting his hand on my shoulder to steady me, as the other sweeps around and presses against my lower back. "You almost toppled over. You okay?"

"I ran into a wall. We'll call it 'Jake.'" I half-laugh and smack his chest with the palm of my hand a few times for good measure. "Seriously. You're like a brick house. Did you know that?"

"It's for the ice," he says, chuckling.

My eyes have stayed focused on him, watching his face, so of course I see the moment he starts looking at *my* lips.

And it's exhilarating.

A warm feeling surges through my veins, and I can feel the heat of his gaze on my skin, sending a flush creeping up my cheeks. Slowly, almost hesitantly, he reaches out a hand, his fingers brushing against mine with a featherlight touch. It's as if he's testing the waters, searching for some sign of permission.

And then, in a heartbeat, everything changes. With a surge of boldness, he closes the gap between us, his lips hovering just inches from mine. The air crackles with anticipation, charged with the promise of what could be...

"Riley! Are you coming out here or what?"

I shoot into the air faster than a firework on the Fourth of July when I hear Levi call my name. We'd barely recovered, with both of us taking a giant leap away from the other, by the time he'd kicked the barn door back open and come inside.

"Come on," he says with a grin, holding up a leash. On the other end is one very happy Becks, who's watching me with excitement in his eyes. "Becks is ready to rock and roll with you two."

"Yeah, sounds good," I mutter, wiping the perspiration off my hands and onto my jeans as I follow Levi out the door. I couldn't even look back at Jake right now if I wanted to, for fear of something inside me imploding. "Ready to go, Jake?"

"You lead and I'll follow," he sings out nonchalantly as the three of us file out of the barn. His words, of course, make my anxious brain click into overdrive wondering if there's a meaning to what he says.

Because there is something to this man that I need to figure out, and I just can't put my finger on what it is.

Yet.

TEN

Jake

Less than twenty-four hours ago and I was almost kissing Riley. Moving through the aisles of the local grocery store, I can admit distraction. You kind of have to when you look into your shopping basket and find you have only managed to get three items on your list, yet you have fifteen or so scribbled on a piece of paper in your hands...and you've been standing in the same spot for almost twenty minutes.

Sighing, I put the can of corn kernels back I'd been staring at and holding onto like a life preserver. It's not even on my list.

Thankfully, my phone rings. I feel like I need the distraction, from my distraction, right now. Glancing at my screen, I smile when I see it's my dad.

"Hey, how are you doing today?"

"Not bad for someone who is getting a little better every day." Hearing the lightness in his voice, I know he's telling me the truth.

"What's on today's agenda—are you still seeing your therapist?"

"Yes, I am. But we're down to two sessions a week." He chuckles. "I promise, I'm in good hands down here without you."

"I wasn't saying that you aren't, I'm just keeping tabs on you."

"You and your tabs. Thank you again for the maid service. I asked the company to pare it back and come only once a week, though. I thought two times a week was overkill."

"Warranted, though?" Diagnosed with hoarding disorder about eighteen months ago, my father has been busy working on himself. That is one good thing about my AHL contract: it allowed me to get my father the help he needed.

"To be fair, yes. But, again, I'm stronger every day." He's quiet for a moment. I get a vision of him sitting in his armchair in his two-bedroom apartment in Sarasota. His place is clean and open, the way he wanted it to be, with tile floors and plenty of sunshine spilling in. "You don't have to always be worried about me now, Jake. I will be better. I am better."

"I know, but you're my dad." It's been just the two of us for so long, and the last few years I'd taken charge of the parent role. How can I explain to him I'm not ready to let it go even though he may be? "Good timing, though. I'm standing in the grocery store staring at the shelves."

"Sounds riveting. Are your contract negotiations going okay?"

"They're going. Hopefully, in the next few days, Travis will get everything lined up."

"You don't sound that excited."

"Well, there's this thing that's happening..."

"A thing?"

"A girl. A woman. There's a woman that's happening to me and I can't shake it, Dad."

"Ahhh, young love. I think I can cast my mind back to those days. Is she all you can think about?"

That and this can of corn. "Yeah."

"When I met your mother, it was almost instantly that I knew she was the one meant for me, but it took us a long time to get together. Mostly because I was so nervous, but also because she was pretty intimidating."

"Really?" Having never really gotten to know my mother, I always tune in when he tells me stories about her. "I've seen pictures of her, she was petite. What was so intimidating?"

"Her presence," he says with a laugh. "She made sure you knew she was in the room just by walking in. Powerful woman and didn't even know it. But, I got over myself and made sure I let her know I was there to win her over."

This is a side of my dad I love getting. "How?"

"I told her. We were friends and in college. There was a group of us who went to dinner one night. Walking back to campus, I lingered at the back of the pack and asked her to walk with me. It was that night I told her my intention was to win her over and do everything in my power to let her see I was the man for her. The one she deserved because I was falling for her."

I could see him doing it, and it made me grin. "What did she say?"

"She laughed at first, but then stopped walking and realized I was serious. From there, the love story began."

"Noted. And also a little scary."

"Did I hear that right? My son, Jake December, being scared?"

"Funny thing is, I think I'm ready for something more in my life." Leaning against the shelf, I drop the basket by my feet. Phone therapy session with my father, aisle nine. "Not that I mean more than hockey, but more than the usual. Like...roots."

"Ah, so you're wanting more than Posh? Hope she handles the news with grace and dignity."

"Aren't you a comedian. But you know what I mean, right?"

"I do. And all I can say is that if you feel in your heart and your soul that this woman is worth the fight, then I'm going to recommend you fight for all it's worth. Having the love of an amazing person on your side, having them in your corner when the going gets rough? That's everything, if you ask me." He then clears his throat. "And, having said the word fight, I think we can segue into why I'm really calling."

I stand up taller. "What's up?"

"Remember when you started playing hockey for that farm team in the Everglades and you had that incident?"

"If by incident, you mean the giant brawl that happened on the ice that one time—"

"—and you ended up in anger management courses because of it. That's the one. Well, I've had a phone call from a reporter this morning who has dug that info up and called me to ask about it."

Heat rises inside of me like a fire that's been ignited, and not in a good way. "Was her name Greta?"

"Sure was," he responds, surprise in his voice. "She said she's a friend of yours and working on a feature article, but she wanted to touch on that. It felt odd to me. If someone was writing a story about you, why bring up the bad things unless they were only trying to dig up the bad?"

"Exactly, Pops." Closing my eyes, I groan. "If she calls again, hang up. Don't respond to anything."

"I'm not sure how you know her, but she was pretty relentless. I kept trying to get off the phone and she actually brought up the time I was in rehabilitation at the psych ward after that incident."

Now, the fire inside? It's raging.

"She did *what*?"

"Don't get stressed, Jake. I just wanted you to know so you

could protect yourself on your end. I'll avoid her on mine, but this sounds like someone who's looking for a story where there isn't one."

"And she's willing to dig out anything she can to make it a front-page headline," I growl. "Tell you what, Dad, let me hang up. I want to call Travis and let him know what's going on. He'll handle it from here. If she calls again, emails, shows up, anything...let me know."

"Immediately. And Jake?"

"Yeah?

"Don't let this ruin that floaty and heady rush I know you're probably feeling right now. There's only one time at the beginning of the relationship that you get to trip and fall in love. Enjoy every step because I think whoever this woman is, she's got you hooked."

"Why do you say that?"

"Because you've never brought up another woman to me before." I can feel his love through the phone lines. "Love you, Jake. Talk soon."

Focusing on my list, I race through the store and get the items I need, including one very important surprise for Riley, then hop into the self-service line and head back outside. Stopping just outside the entrance, I scan the small parking lot, trying to remember where I parked.

Spotting the familiar white Fiat at the back of the lot, I head that way, threading through cars, when someone calls my name. I'm by the rack where people return their grocery carts when I stop and turn around.

Standing next to a small minivan, wearing a Renegades jersey with my number on it, is Mandy.

"Hey, Jake," she calls out again, turning around so I can see my name on the back of her jersey. She spins around to face me, grinning. "Like it?"

"Yeah, that's cool, Mandy. Thanks for your support," I say, flicking my hand in the air as I start to walk away. "See you."

"Wait," she calls out, running up beside me and placing herself in my path. "I was serious the other day when I was asking you about the private lessons. Is it something you'd be interested in?"

"I'm not here long enough to do that," I begin, but she's not having any of it.

"I'll pay you well," she purrs, placing her hand on my arm. Her touch doesn't have the soothing effect I'm sure she intended. Instead, it makes me flinch and I jump back a step.

"Sorry, Mandy. It's not a good idea." Tilting my chin toward my car, I raise my bags in the air. "I really need to go."

Once again, I'm walking toward the car, and once again, Mandy appears in front of me, this time putting her hand on my chest to stop me.

"Wait." She pulls a piece of paper out of her pocket. When I look closer, I realize it's a business card. "My number's on this. Should you choose to call it."

We then stand for another uncomfortable minute in the parking lot. With my hands full gripping groceries, she tucks the card into my back pocket with one hand and taps my chest with the other. She steps back, with this eerie grin on her face.

This is just weird.

"Okay, Mandy, thanks." I take a giant step away from her and make a beeline for the car. "I really have to go."

I don't even take a moment to look behind me to make sure she's not following me. I swap one of the bags over so I'm clutching them in one hand while the other fishes in my pocket for the keys.

Once I'm safely inside my car, I shake my head as I look around the parking lot and make sure Mandy's cleared the area. I've dealt with pushy fans before, but having one place their hands on me in public is a first.

Most importantly, though, I have learned something from this run-in with her.

There's only one woman I want to see wearing my jersey... and it's not Mandy.

ELEVEN

Riley

"So you got a dog and managed to almost kiss the sworn enemy."

"I wouldn't call him the enemy," I say, standing up and shielding my eyes from the midday sun. The Sweetkiss Creek Dog Park isn't too busy today, which is good for me. I wanted to bring Becks here so I could start getting him socialized. Luckily, I have a couple of girlfriends with dogs, so they agreed to come, too...and apparently they also brought their friends Judgement and Opinion, too.

"You said you never wanted to date or deal with hockey players again," Dylan manages to say while laughing. She whistles, calling her terrier, Max, back up the hill with Becks and Toto, Georgie's Rottweiler, trailing along after him. "You're dealing with one to the point that your lips almost touched."

"But she says he has some sexy tattoos," Georgie says conspiratorially, winking at Dylan. "That's pretty big stuff right there."

"Wow, talk about reading into things." Giggling, I cross my arms and turn around to face the pair, leaning against one another on the park bench in quiet hysterics. I point a finger at

Dylan. "I expected you to be a little more open to this idea, considering I was one of your besties who helped you figure out you were in love with your best friend." Taking a sweeping bow, I put on my best fake British accent. "You're welcome, by the way."

"She has a point," Georgie agrees. "And it is kind of cool that you and your best friend are now husband and wife."

"But we're not talking about me," Dylan says, her tone clipped as she points a finger back my way. "We're talking about the commitment-phobe here, the woman who loves her turtle and was forced by one of her oldest friends to get a dog."

I roll my eyes. "It's a trial basis, anyway."

"Jake?" Georgie asks.

"Becks," I say, smacking her playfully. "Levi texted me that he would take him back if it didn't work out." When he'd made the offer the other night, it had made it a little easier to settle in with Becks, I'll admit, but watching him run down the hill with Max and Toto beside him, his tongue hanging out the side of his mouth and basically smiling, there's no way I'll ever take this away from him. "However, I also invested a nice chunk of change in a memory-foam dog bed so he could sleep like a rockstar, now that he's retired from truffle farming at an early age. And he's really cute."

No sooner are the words out of my mouth than Becks tears up the hill, stopping on a pin at my feet, and leaning his full body weight against me. Sighing with pleasure, I glance over at my friends, who are both watching like a proud mama bird whose baby took flight from the nest.

"Look, Dylan," Georgie whispers. "It's responsibility and she's taking it so well."

"I know. It's very sweet to see." She turns to Georgie, placing her hands on her lap like she's a lady of high society at tea. "And she may also be opening her heart to possibilities, too. It's like a first-quarter of the year miracle."

"Har, har. Look, my side hurts I'm laughing so hard," I say as flatly as I can. As the two smack each other on the leg and laugh at their own stupid jokes, I shake my head and scratch Becks behind his ears. "Earmuffs, sweetie. This is when we ignore them. They're like the two little old men in the balcony of the Muppet Show."

"I still need to see that show," Georgie murmurs as she stands up and stretches her arms over her head. "Anyone know what time it is?"

I reach into my back pocket to check the time, and I'm more than a little surprised when I see I've got a text...from someone I don't want to hear from.

"You guys," I say, holding my cell phone. "Todd messaged me."

Dylan's eyes widen. "What?"

"Read it," Georgie demands. She's bossy, this one.

I tap open the bubble and scan the message. I get two words in when Georgie huffs. "I meant out loud."

Acquiescing, I sigh and begin. "Riley, you've been in my thoughts a lot lately. I haven't felt right about how things ended and I want a chance to make it up to you, if you'll let me. We'll be playing in Virginia next week. If you're open to talking, please let me know and I'll get you tickets to the game. Maybe you could wear my jersey?" Pulling my eyes up to meet the two pairs watching me, I gag. "He added a little winky face at the end there, but come on. How narcissistic do you need to be? Little does he know I gave his jersey away."

"Delete, delete, delete," Dylan says, wiping her hands in the air. "We all know you're better than that. Is he still sending flowers, too?"

"He sent a bouquet a few days ago; I gave those to Frannie," I say with a shrug. "But they tapered off, finally. Figured if I didn't acknowledge them, he'd get the hint."

"Introducing you to his family at Thanksgiving, then

showing up in a magazine with his new girlfriend two weeks later, right before Christmas, is like...nasty. Icky. Sleazy, smarmy—"

Holding up a hand, I cut Georgie off. "I get it. It's yuck and I agree. He is yuck."

"But Jake..."

Dylan never gets to finish because I cut my eyes her way and put a finger to my lips. "The first rule about dating club is you don't talk about dating club."

"Pfft," Georgie makes a sound with her mouth as she gets up and calls Toto over to her. "You have to have a real date for a date to happen. This is more like crush club."

"I like that. Crush Club—where single ladies can live in their heads crushing on the man they want and never get close. That way it stays a perfect relationship in their mind, full of chemistry and tension, none of the real stuff."

"You need a therapist." Dylan tosses Beck's leash at me, which I sidestep while laughing. "But she's got a point. Maybe you could just dip your toes in with a date while he's here."

"A date?"

Georgie's eyes light up. "Yes! Oh my gosh, that's brilliant. In fact, I think we should make it mandatory."

"Great idea." Dylan spins around to face Georgie and they high-five. She then turns back to me. "In fact, we're going to break the mold here. You, Riley Richards, are going to ask HIM out on a date."

There are dips in our tummies when we get nervous, like when you're waiting for test results or being pulled over by the police when you know you weren't speeding, then there are the kinds of dips you get when you jump from a plane or are maybe doing something that is, in your mind, equivalent to that action. This particular nervous dip is more like a flurry of delicate but chaotic movements in my stomach. Erratic motions causing a jumble of sensations that feel just shy of awful. "I have to do what?"

"Ask him out. It can be any kind of date you want, but put yourself out there. You were happy to sit back and just be in a 'thing' with Todd, but look where it got you."

"Heartbreak," Georgie answers.

"Exactly," Dylan acknowledges. "You've always sat back and not taken control of your love life. There was the time you liked that guy in the police department and he wanted to date you, too. I think it was Tim?"

Cringing at the thought, I nod. "I remember."

"He wanted to ask you out, but you were so aloof and nonchalant, he took it that you weren't interested and he eventually moved on."

"I wanted him to think I was a challenge?" I say, making a face because I'm not even sure why I acted like that. Sometimes, I feel stunted when it comes to love. Like I'll never get it right, and obviously, my time with Tim was one of my not-so-finest moments.

"Well, your challenge is to ask this man out and get to know him. He obviously wants to get to know you if he almost kissed ya." Dylan then looks at her watch. "And it's almost one-thirty, Georgie. Am I dropping you back off at the bookshop?"

"Please," she responds as we all gather our four-legged babies. "Am I keeping Becks tonight while you go to your parents' house for the trial meal?"

"Yes, please and thank you." I hand the leash over to Georgie. "I'll pick him up after I'm done. Cross your fingers, ladies. I hope Mom is happy with what I've got planned."

"I'm not even worried about her." Dylan wags her finger at me as she walks toward her car. "I'm worried about you. You. Be open to possibility. You are a catch, and so what if he's a hockey player? If he's making you get excited about the idea of kissing someone, then I say go for it. Life is pretty rough these days, and if we get these little glimmers appearing to make us forget what a dumpster fire things can be, how amazing is that? It's like dreaming, but you're wide awake at the same time."

"That's also called a sleeping pill overdose," Georgie jokes, nudging Dylan in the ribs. "Let's go...and good luck tonight, Riley. I'll see you after."

Watching two of my best friends in the world walk away, I have to admit that I feel better after talking to them. Stronger. Empowered even. Now I need to tell that to my nerves, because the thought of asking Jake on a date makes me want to pee myself.

Standing beside my childhood dining room table, I'm sweating. It's hot in the kitchen, it's hot in the dining room, and my mom's attitude has me hot under the collar. She barely approved of the appetizer, but thanks to my father, he convinced her it was a pass. And now she's onto my wild mushroom and sage chicken with a creamy truffle sauce, I feel exposed.

She slowly puts the fork to her mouth, takes a bite, and chews. And chews.

And. Chews.

"Wow," Dad says, his eyes gleaming as he looks at me. "That's incredible, Riley."

"Thanks, Dad."

"To be fair, your father also thought you were doing well when you painted the wall by your crib with your own poop when you were a baby." My mother, her tone dry, gives him a look as the door to the kitchen swings open behind me.

"Poop?" Travis says, a grin playing on his lips as he enters the room, with one Jake December hot on his heels. "Did I hear the poop story being brought up again?"

I cover my face with my hands. "Can we not do this? At least not now."

"Because you have company?" Jake asks, jumping in. Not only has his entrance shocked me, but his sudden joining in of the family tease does as well.

"No, because these two are eating and I don't want to take anything away from the meal." Realizing Travis is here and not in New York, I tilt my head to the side. "What are you doing at home, anyway?"

"More contract negotiations," he says, patting Jake on the back. "We're close to having this guy back on his old team. Just a few more details to nail down. So, back to the poop…"

"Shut it, Travis." Rolling my eyes, I turn back to my mother. "Seriously. How is it?"

She nods. "It's not bad. A little salty for my taste, but it's okay."

"Okay?" Beside her, my father is almost done with his main course. "I give it a five out of four stars, it's that good."

"You'd give a quarter-pounder with cheese five stars if you could." Mom laughs.

"But good enough for dinner?" I press.

"Yes, sweetie, it is good enough." She pushes her plate away, looking back at me expectantly. "Dessert?"

"I did a spin on things," I say over my shoulder as I head toward the kitchen. "Talk amongst yourselves and I'll be out in a second with the finale."

In the kitchen, I go to the cupboard and pull out a platter to arrange the chocolate truffles I'd made that day on, waiting to hear the familiar swoosh of the door closing behind me. Only it doesn't.

When I turn around, I find Jake standing in the doorway, holding the door open.

"Need help?"

"Nah, I'm okay," I say, turning my back to him as a tingle of heat travels up my spine. Thinking about my earlier talk with my friends, I close my eyes and take a breath. Maybe asking for help isn't a bad idea.

"Actually," I say, turning back around—in time to see he's about to return to the dining room—I point to the fridge. "I'd love your help. Can you please grab the container of chocolate truffles out of the refrigerator for me?"

Jake grins and throws me a mock salute. "Aye, aye. Is that what I say to a chef?"

Cracking up, I shake my head and turn away to focus. "More like 'yes, chef,' but I'll take aye, aye."

In a flash, he's beside me and slides the container over in front of me. I peel back the lid, and we're hit with a wave of chocolate aroma.

Jake, who is standing close enough that I can smell the shampoo he used this morning, leans in closer and points to one of the round sugar bomb-like white truffles. His head is at an angle so that as he speaks, each word hits the back of my neck like the tiniest whisper of a kiss and it sends a thrill to my very core.

"So, these are regular dessert truffles, right? There's no mushroomy truffle parts in them?"

Mint. His breath is minty with a touch of coffee on its edge, and it's like catnip to me. My body naturally leans into his as I turn my head so we're in each other's line of sight, side by side, at the counter.

"Exactly. I made a few that are your run-of-the-mill chocolate truffles, like this one," I say, pointing to them. Reaching down, I grab one, plucking it from the container and holding it out to Jake. "Want to try?"

We're close enough that I can see the golden flecks dancing in his dark brown eyes. When I inhale, I can taste him on the tip of my tongue, and that's saying something for proximity. I'm also wanting to check my own breath, thinking back to the bean and onion burrito I horked down on the way over, but never mind.

"Please," he whispers, opening his mouth but keeping his eyes locked on mine. Swallowing, I realize he wants me to feed him, so I take my cue. Because nothing has ever felt sexier to me than this very moment. I'm caught in some kind of romantic movie scene and don't want anyone to pull me out.

Lifting the truffle, I slowly and carefully place it on his lips, and he reaches up and wraps his fingers around my wrist as I do, steadying me. My jaw wants to slacken, but I'm fighting it, attempting to keep my cool. But the simplicity of this man staring into my eyes as he eats food from my fingers, food that I made no less, is stirring up a whir of feelings inside me I didn't know existed.

His lips wrap around the truffle, encasing it as he uses his teeth and gently takes it from my hand. His lips momentarily grazed across my skin and send a heady rush, a sensation of fire raging through my system. And in the next second, his eyes are closed and he leans against me, groaning as he chews.

"What kind of sorcery is this?" he mutters, eyes still closed and mouth full as he shifts his weight and leans against the counter now, using both hands. "It's melting inside my mouth."

"Good. That's what I wanted," I say, oh so softly while I stare at his lips, again. My new favorite pastime. Beautiful, smooth pink lips that have a fleck of chocolate on the edges. A part of me resists the urge to reach out and brush my lips across his.

Inhaling sharply, I try to calm my breath as I lick my own lips, but Jake's eyes snap open when I do so. His eyes flick to my lips, then back up so he's holding my gaze, a tiny smile beginning to ripple.

"Are you looking at my mouth, Riley?" he asks, his voice hushed as he leans in closer.

"Well," I say, still whispering, with a nod. I then point to the corner of my mouth. "You've got something. Here."

"Oh." He chuckles and wipes a hand across his mouth, but somehow misses the crumble. "Did I get it?"

"No." I giggle, pointing again, but this time to his face. "It's there."

Swiping again, he looks at me expectantly. But no dice. "It's still there."

"Obviously I can't see it." Jake shoves his face closer to mine. "Do you mind helping a guy out?"

Swallowing again, I give an internal speech to my nerves, shutting them up as I reach out and gently, using my thumb, wipe the chocolate off his face. As I pull my hand away, Jake looks down and sees the chocolate that's transferred itself from its location onto my skin now.

"I don't like wasting things." Taking my hand, and still keeping his eyes locked with mine, I watch in slow motion as Jake lightly places his mouth onto the very tip of my thumb, licking the chocolate off, before he smacks his lips together and grins.

Everything inside of me hitches. I'm not prepared for any of this. My homework was to ask him out, and now, this man is in front of me licking my fingers.

I. Cannot. Cope.

I'm fighting a solo argument in my head. There is something in this moment that feels so good. Warm. Amazing. Even if we are in the kitchen of my childhood home.

My family. Oh yeah.

Remembering them, I try to turn my attention back to plating the desert, but Jake's got other ideas. He looks around the room and finds something he's looking for. He then takes my hand and pulls me toward the pantry.

My mind is screaming *BRAKES!* but my body steps on the gas. "What are you..."

"I think you want some powdered sugar to put on your truffles?" he says with a wink.

"No." Who would do that? "I would never..."

"Riley. Stop talking." Wrapping his arms around me, he pulls me in close as he pushes my hair away from my eyes. "I'm going to kiss you now, mostly to get you to stop talking. Is that okay?"

"Well, yes, but..." I can't even argue any points. It only takes him a moment, and it is oh-so-slow and oh-so-sweet, as his lips slant across mine and everything in me explodes. There's a specific feeling that comes up for me as he pulls me in so my body is firmly against his.

Jake's movements are slow, strategic, and gentle, his hands sliding up and down my arms as I revel in the tension crackling in the air around us. He pulls away for a moment so we can catch our breath, but I can see it in his eyes as he gazes upon me, his eyelids heavy as he drags his eyes from mine to my lips and back again.

"Riley?" he asks, as if he needs to question the moment and ask permission again. I don't say a word; instead, I reach out and tug on his shirt, pulling him close to me yet again and landing his lips on top of mine.

There's no hesitation, no slowing down now. His lips are soft and warm, like Kryptonite for me. So, so bad, but I only want more. I can feel his heart racing against my chest as we press harder against each other's bodies. His hand cradles my neck, holding me in the perfect position so I can also wrap my arms around his waist and grip his shirt tighter in my grasp and bring him in and against me, more.

For a moment, we're suspended in time and nothing is moving except us, our lips, and our hands, and it's so delicious.

We stay here, in our own little world for a moment before I finally slow things down and pull myself away. We're like this for just a second, our foreheads touching, as we catch our breaths.

"Um..." I clear my throat, untangling myself from his arms as I smooth out my shirt. "I was going to ask you if you'd like to go out for a coffee and dessert tonight. But we kind of skipped the whole date first, kiss later thing."

"I want nothing more than to go out with you to anything, anywhere tonight," he whispers, wrapping an arm around my waist and pulling me back against his chest. His eyes bounce between mine as he grins. "Riley, you are..."

"Hey, Riley," Travis's voice shakes us both out of our reverie. "What's up with the sugar, sugar?"

"They're coming." I fall out from the pantry first, smoothing my hair back as I walk over to where I'd left the truffles. "It's coming. I-I was looking for some extra chocolate for shavings, but..."

Glancing at Travis, I'm in time to witness the look of confusion followed by realization cross his face when Jake exits the pantry behind me. I want to act like nothing just happened, but even I know that the electricity in the air right now is palpable, and Travis would have to be a darn fool to not feel it.

But I'll try anyway.

"I made Jake help me," I begin, but Travis shakes his head.

"Dude." He crosses his arms and sets Jake in his sights, a look of shock flashing across his features. "Were you really in the pantry just now with my sister?"

S eeing Jake turn six shades of pale white makes my hands twitch nervously. My eyes bounce back and forth between Travis and Jake, a feeling of nausea beginning to rise.

Note to self: take into account that you're kissing your brother's best friend next time. Also, your brother's client. It's like I jammed a little family and a touch of business with a scoop of personal pleasure into a blender and hit the button, turning it on high without thinking.

I can't lie. His kiss was ridiculously amazing, but seeing the skewed expression on my brother's face is making me question my own sanity at the moment.

"So?" Travis inclines his chin at the pantry door. "Were you two just in there, together, or am I seeing things?" He then glances over at me and makes a sweeping motion with his hand from the tip of my head to my feet. "And you look like a flustered mess. I mean, Mom is definitely putting you through the paces, but I know you can recover from her guff. You've got a weird look on your face. Guilty."

"Okay, I'm sorry," Jake says, stepping forward. "I know

what I just did wasn't cool, man. We were—I was in the pantry and..."

I can feel Jake's anxiety, it's dripping off each word he speaks. I want to pick at my fingernails, that's how anxious I am, but I keep my breath slow and steady.

"So you were in a small space together." Travis nods, and I think I see a flicker of laughter sweep across his features. I take a second to glance back at Jake, who meets my look with worry in his eyes. I know what my brother's friendship means to him; he told me as much.

My eyes then rock to Travis, who at this point is clearly having a good time at our expense. A huge grin takes over as he shakes his head and leans forward, clapping Jake on his back.

"I'm only kidding. What you two do is none of my business," Travis says, but he stops laughing and goes serious real quick. "I will say, because it's my job as her brother, that if you do anything to hurt her or break her heart, I may hurt you."

"Oh my...Travis!" I'm the one shaking my head now. "Stop it. We're not...anything. We're, well. We're trying out a thing where—"

Travis laughs. "You're tongue-tied and his face is bright red. And you're going to try to convince me nothing is going on? You were always a terrible liar, Riley."

"We're in 'no comment' territory," Jake says, coming to my rescue. "But, noted on everything you said."

Travis nods and points a finger at him. "As long as we understand each other. I came in here to let you know I just got an email. You're back with the Renegades, it's official."

"Seriously?" Jake exclaims as he claps his hands together and jumps in the air. "That's amazing. Thank you, Travis, so much!"

Jake then surprises both of us by lunging at Travis and pulling him into a bear hug. "This is the best news."

Laughing, Travis pulls away. "You have some smoothing

over to do, but I'll leave it in your capable hands. Didn't you say that Henry reached out to you recently?"

As the two guys put their heads together and get into hockey-speak, the door to the dining room swings open and my mother flies in. The only thing that's missing is her broom.

"Are you bringing the dessert truffles out or is it a self-service kind of thing, like a buffet?"

"Sorry," I mumble, tossing the last one on the plate for her. It's not my finest presentation, but I've been distracted. Very, very distracted and I liked it. "Here. I did a play on the whole truffle theme and made sweet truffles for dessert."

She eyes the plate, hovering her hand over a white chocolate truffle, which she finally picks up. I'm a little surprised when she places it under her nostrils and takes a whiff.

"What are you doing?"

"Seeing if I can smell any surprise ingredients." She then winks at me. "I know you like to punch up your recipes with extra flavor."

Something I had no idea that she even knew about me. "Really?"

"Yes, sweetie," Mom says as she puts her free arm around me. "I love the cinnamon kick that comes with your chocolate croissants. And the slap I got from the truffle sauce with your chicken was interesting."

My little heart is going to explode. It could also implode. It's just going to blow up because I can't believe I'm getting these compliments right now. And it's not that she doesn't tell me I do a good job at things, it's just that she's usually my harshest critic, especially when it comes to cooking. Okay, maybe harsh is too strong of a word. She's my most vocal critic?

"Then you're going to like the white chocolate truffles," I say with a wink. "They're laced with the essence of key lime."

Jake and Travis are still chatting away as she pops it in her mouth. She chews for a moment before slapping the counter with her hand. "Oh. My. Gawwwd...that is to die for, Riley James Richards!"

Blushing, I turn to the two guys and then point to my mom. "Did you hear that?"

"That she called you James?" Jake says.

"No," Travis corrects. "She got the full-name treatment. That means 'you done good' in our house."

My hand slaps my brother's in an epic sibling high-five before we turn in a circle and bump our hips together. It's the Richards kids' dance of happiness, and we've not done that in a long time.

"What are you doing?" Jake asks, but no one is listening. My mother is still moaning as she swallows the sugary concoction I created.

"That was heaven, my dear. You're going to kill it at the dinner." She grabs another truffle from the plate, this one milk chocolate. "Do you have a server helping you?"

"Ah, no," I say, my happiness suddenly crashing when I see the look of disappointment wash over her face. "But I can find one. No problem at all. I'm sure Georgie can help."

My mother's stern expression is back. I feel like she's judging me for this one item I've not handled. "Just make sure they get the full treatment. Your reputation is mine, got it?"

"Got it."

"Well, we're all done, then. Let me know how it goes." She then turns to Travis. "Your father wants to see you before you take off."

She heads back out to the dining room, with Travis right behind her. He stops at the door, then turns back to me.

"Don't let her get to you. She told me it was excellent. She just wants you to do a good job because she loves you. Okay?" He then waves to Jake. "Talk to you later this week. We'll sort out the details tomorrow, cool?"

As the door swings shut, I turn to face Jake, who is starting to laugh. I throw a towel at him, which he ducks, of course.

"So can we go out now?" he asks, his tone teasing.

"Help me get this place cleaned up, and then I'm free."

Cleaning the kitchen and loading my car took no time flat with both of us doing it. If I'm not mistaken, I think Jake was going faster than a normal person would, but I know I was, too. One moment of weakness in a food pantry and now all I want to do is get those lips on mine again.

Back in town, I park near the fountain. Jake spots the ice cream shop that's still open, so we order an ice cream cone each and then make our way back over to our fountain and sit on its edge.

I like thinking it's our fountain, even though we've only sat on it together one other time. Before he sits down, Jake suddenly pops up and jogs back to the ice cream shop, returning a moment later jangling a few loose coins in his hand.

When he sees my quizzical expression, he opens his hand, showing me the dimes scattered on his palm.

"For wishes." He's so matter-of-fact, like I should have known. And it's adorable.

"Is this really the guy who Sports Center said was a bomb of anger ready to explode?" I ask.

"They got it wrong, obviously," he chuckles, licking his ice cream. "I'm the first to admit I can be moody. But the day I got into the fight with my teammate was more about morals and principles than anything else."

I can see my opening to tell him about Todd, but there's something in his demeanor that tells me he wants to keep talking. I feel like Jake is akin to the best piece of candy out there that you can find: it's coated in a thick chocolate shell that's impenetrable. It's hard and crusty, maybe even a little bit thicker than you'd like, but when you break it open and get to its warm, caramel, gooey center, it's worth all of the wait and the work behind it. So I stay quiet and eat my ice cream.

"I'm not proud of it, you know," he says, dark brown eyes slamming into mine. "But, this guy is such a tool. He spent a lot of practice time talking about his conquests."

A feeling of sick hits the back of my throat. "Conquests?"

"He's a serial dater. He was dating two girls at one time, could have been a third in the mix, but none of them knew about each other." Jake leans forward, elbows on his knees as he stares at the round. "I knew there was one he was dating that was long distance, but the other two were locals. I'd see them at games or out with him at dinner sometimes. And it just was...weird."

Curiosity starts to get the better of me. "When was this?"

"Let me think..." Jake pauses. "You know, he was dating all of these women at the same time, around three months ago, but I didn't say anything until two weeks ago. That's when the fight happened."

I do the math, and a mix of sadness and surprise kicks me in the gut realizing that I'm most likely the long-distance woman he's talking about.

"So you didn't like that he was seeing all these people at once, but you waited to bring it up?"

"It's not that I bought it up, he started talking in the locker room about them. He was down to one girlfriend a few weeks ago, but then she got wise and dumped him. The guys were teasing him, and so he was bragging that he could win back one of his other women 'on the bench.'" Jake shakes his head. "He actually ordered flowers to be delivered to one of them that night in front of us. And the card he sent with it.

Oy." Jake cringes. "So cheesy. I heard enough and told him to stop."

"Why?" Because now I have to know.

"Because they're not just faceless women, but someone's daughter or sister. They're people who shouldn't be handled like tokens in a game. There's something to be said about winning someone over, but in this case, he just wanted to be a winner. It made me despise him and what he stood for, and I lost faith in my teammate."

The fact that the sequence of events and the timeline all feel exceptionally close to what I'd gone through was eerie. And the arrival of the flowers and the more frequent apology texts from Todd? Now they make sense. The coincidence that it's Jake who was at the heart of this, or maybe it's serendipitous...I'm not sure.

Time to come clean in case I pass out.

"I know Todd," I say softly, licking my ice cream for good measure. "I dated him until a few months ago when I found out, thanks to a photo in a magazine, that he was in a relationship with someone named Shelly."

His jaw slack, Jake does a double take. "Shelly?"

I nod. "I have a feeling I'm the long-distance girl you're talking about. In fact, he started sending me flowers a few weeks ago and texting me every few days, trying to get me to talk to him."

A look of irritation flashes on his face, but Jake calms himself and his reaction, and he only nods his head. "What are the odds?"

"I think we should play a lottery ticket, that's the kind of odds we're looking at," I say, attempting to make a joke. "You got into a fight with him on the ice and off, right?"

"I was mad when we went out on the ice because of his attitude and lack of remorse. It just felt gross. Then he bumped me when we got out there. I'm sure he meant nothing from it, but it made me madder. So, I hit him."

The way Jake throws his hands in the air makes me laugh, but I turn serious quickly. "But you kept fighting."

"Yeah." Eyes downcast, he takes a bite of his cone. "At the end of the game, he came up to me and started poking me in the chest with his finger, just inciting things. He was mad that I had acted the way I did, and I was mad, too. I was about to say I was sorry when he got aggressive, and it didn't help things. I reacted and...well, it's history now. I was suspended and now I'm heading back to my old team."

"But you're okay with going back there?"

"I am. I left there in a blaze of glory, but I'll save you that tale for another day." He chuckles. "Right now, James, I want to give you something. Close your eyes and open your hand."

"You can't use my middle name against me, ever, you know." I close my eyes as he's reaching into his pocket. I had admitted to him on the ride over that my middle name was an odd one, the result of my parents thinking they were getting a boy. Surprise. I showed up.

I keep my eyes closed tightly until, a moment later, there's a small package placed in the palm of my hand. The packaging makes a crackling sound, and while it's an odd shape, it's a familiar one.

"Can I look now?" I say, holding up my prize.

"Go ahead."

Opening one eye, I peek at my hand, giggling when I see it. I tear open the plastic and pluck the candy ring out. I take a quick lick before smiling and looking back at Jake. "It's watermelon flavored! My favorite."

"I had to get it when I saw it." He takes the ring from me and takes my hand. "Let me do the honors."

I watch in stunned silence as he places the candy ring on

my ring finger. Okay, so no, it's not a ring that means anything, but COME ON! How romantic is it to be sitting by a fountain on a spring evening with a cute boy who you just found out stood up for you…and he didn't even know you at the time?

I think I've fallen into a fairytale. If this guy can sing, then I'm definitely in a Disney film. One hundred percent.

He must have had a similar thought because his eyes began a slow procession upward, finding mine again. We hold our gaze for a second before he clears his throat and, grinning, runs his fingers through his hair.

"Well," he says before he pops the last of his ice cream cone into his mouth. "I hate to break this up, but I need to practice early tomorrow. I want to be ready so I can hopefully play in the last games of the season with the Renegades."

"No, I get it," I say, popping the last of my ice cream in my mouth, taking a quick lick of my ring to show my appreciation as well. "And thanks for the jewelry."

Holding out his hand to help me stand, he looks at the ring on my finger, stroking the back of my hand with his thumb. "It looks good."

"Don't forget," I say, poking him in the ribs. "You've got change. Are we wishing for anything?"

"Yes!" Jake exclaims, grabbing the change from his pocket and putting a dime in my hand. He closes his eyes, tosses his coin, and looks back at me once it breaks the surface. "I was ready with a wish. Your turn."

"That was the fastest wish in the west," I manage to say, giggling. I close my eyes and a thousand wishes come to mind. I wish that my dinner would go well, I wish that I could kiss Jake again, but I also wish for the world to be perfect and peaceful for everyone in it. So, yeah.

Keeping my eyes closed, I toss my coin, opening my eyes when I hear the *kerplunk* sound as it hits the water. When I open my eyes, I see someone that I did not wish for across the square, peering around the fountain watching us.

Jake's gaze follows mine, and he clocks Mandy across the way with her arms crossed. He quickly turns back to me.

"Look, I'm sorry, but she's been impossible. She's a stage-one clinger and it's really uncomfortable, especially since she's married."

"Well," I say, threading my arms around his neck as I step closer to him. "Looks like we need to nip this in the bud."

"Am I allowed to pull you in like this?" Jake wraps his arms around my waist and he pulls my body tight against his. "Maybe if she sees us like this, she won't try to get my attention anymore."

"Hmmm, I'm not sure about that," I retort. Honestly, I don't know who this Riley is, but she's sassy and flirty, and she's taking no prisoners. I let my eyes drift to his lips, then back to his eyes, hoping he gets my message. "I think there are other methods we can utilize to make her think you're...off the market, shall we say?"

"You don't have to tell me twice." His fingers dig into the soft flesh of my hips as his mouth comes down across mine. And I'm just done.

At this moment, I don't care that he's a hockey player, and I don't care about my stupid old rules. I don't care that Mandy is watching, and I definitely don't care that Todd broke my heart because I can feel clearly that it's mended.

It's the second time today that Jake's pulled me into his arms and kissed me like I've never been kissed before, and it's showstopping. It's a stop the presses, we've got a new headline type of kiss. His lips are the kind of thing that makes history—at least it will go down in my memory banks as the best kiss ever.

EVER.

One of us has to stay focused on the fact that we are in

public, so I slow things down and start to pull away, slowly untangling myself from his warmth. We both take a moment to laugh, little nervous ones, if I'm not mistaken. My hand flies to my lips in sweet shock as we both look around.

And Mandy's nowhere to be seen.

THIRTEEN

Jake

Yesterday was the day that will go down in the history books as the day I kissed Riley Richards. Twice. Two times, people. In one day. There were two times that my lips were on hers, and it was amazing. Blissful. Full of promise.

Addictive. I want more.

Today is the day that I'm lying on her old bed, in her old bedroom, in her parents' house thinking about the fact that when I go downstairs to do anything, I will be carrying the pleasurable guilt of having made out with their daughter.

That kitchen pantry will never look the same.

Rolling over, I stick my legs out straight from under the covers and throw my hands above my head to get a full-body stretch flowing. Something at my feet jumps, straddling me for a second until sloppy doggy kisses remind me that my main woman is in need of my attention.

"Here, girl." Cooing, I wrap my arm around her and pull her close. Posh closes her little eyes, sighs a happy doggie sound, and lays down with me, falling back to sleep almost immediately. Stroking the spot between her ears slowly, wondering what it'll be like when she gets to meet Becks.

I sit up straight in bed, again scaring my girl to the point she jumps up and glares my way. Posh. Becks.

Posh.

Becks.

What are the odds? Could our dogs be showing us the sign that we're supposed to be together?

Laughing at my ridiculousness, I fling myself back down on my pillows and grab my phone from the bedside table to check emails and messages. One email makes my hair stand on end. It's to Greta and it's from Travis, but he's copied my lawyer and someone else at her publication. The subject line is "Cease and Desist."

Tapping a few buttons, it's only a ring or two in when Travis answers.

"Guess you saw the email."

Do I tell him I was in the middle of daydreaming about kissing his little sister when I did? Nah. Not this time. I like my teeth. "I did. Has she responded?"

"Not yet. I'll let you know when she does. Until then, just ignore any articles and tell your dad to hang in there. If she tries to call again, he can hang up and let us know. We'll handle it from here."

"Thanks, man," I say, pulling Posh onto my lap. She's passed out again and snuggled down into my arms. "I owe you. A lot."

"And yet you thank me by kissing my sister," he points out. "Remember that?"

Groaning, I slap my hand to my forehead. "Travis. Man. I am so sorry, I don't know what happened..."

"I do." He chuckles. "And look, I'm only kidding, but I meant what I said yesterday. She's still my little sister, and if you do anything that hurts her, I will have to step up and do my brother job."

"I get it." Tracing a tiny path through Posh's coat, I stare out the bedroom window. "She's really cool, and I can't explain why, but I'm pulled to her. Like a magnet."

"Okay, I don't need to hear about any of this," he says, but for some reason, I feel the need to explain myself.

"I can't call it insta-love, 'cause I don't know if that's what it is, but there are some insta-feelings happening that I've not had before."

"Don't you have some girls who are friends you can talk to about this?" he asks.

I love when Travis gets uncomfortable. I may be a wall of hidden emotion, but with me, the well runs deep and when I'm ready to let you see that side of me, I'm an open book. But Travis? He's pent-up. After meeting his mother, I'm starting to understand where he gets it from.

"You're the closest I have right now," I say, laughing. "But I am going to call Henry to see how things are at the Renegades. Feel him out for what the other guys are saying."

I can almost see Travis's pleased expression now. Pleased that I changed the subject and super pleased I'm reaching out to my old teammates.

"Love that. I'm talking to the assistant coach today and he's going to let me know what day you're back on the roster. I have a feeling they want to keep it quiet, then spring it on the local fans a day or two before your first game back. I bet the ticket sales go off."

He's quiet for a moment before continuing, "Look, when it comes to Riley, I'm always going to be a little bit protective, but she is her own woman now. She's been hurt before, and as her family, we can't stand to see that pain. But smiling Riley is another story, and my parents have said that she's doing more of that lately than she has in a long time. She's our sunshine, Jake. Got it?"

This is for sure the closest thing I'm going to get in the way of having permission to do anything with his sister. There's a warm feeling inside of me, an acceptance that eases fears I didn't know I had.

"Loud and clear." Clearing my throat, I glance at the clock on the dresser across the room and hop out of bed. "I need to hit the rink to do some drills. Should I check in later?"

"Nah, I've got it. I'll reach out if I have anything for you. But call Henry, and be good to my sis."

Disconnecting the call, I throw on an old pair of sweats and my Renegades zip-up hoodie as I grab my bag of equipment and gear. Sliding my phone in my pocket, I slip downstairs for breakfast so I can grab a bite and head out.

It's quiet in the Richards house, which means I can move at my pace and not engage. It also gives me time to look at the family photos on the wall, most especially the ones of Riley in various poses: from her high school graduation (where she's surrounded by a ton of people, including Levi and Austin), to what looks like a new car. There's more with various family members and tons of her and Travis, signaling the closeness of these two that I already knew.

The thought of their family unit and the love it provides makes me happy inside. and for once, not jealous of what someone else has as far as a home life. Seeing the interactions here with the Richards makes me realize that while it was only Dad and I growing up, he did his best to make sure I never felt alone.

Grabbing a bowl from a kitchen cabinet, I fling open the pantry door and step inside, only to shiver as the memory of her lips on mine, right here in this small space, not that long ago, floods back.

All I know is that I'm ready for a repeat.

Sitting by the concession stand at the arena, I'm about to tuck into one of Riley's world-famous in Sweetkiss Creek croissants when my phone rings. Seeing Henry's name flash on the screen, I make sure to grab it instantly.

"I'm glad you called," I say between bites.

"When you wake up to a text that says 'we need to talk' you make time out to call one of your oldest friends," he says. "Are the rumors true, December? Freedom ain't nothing 'cause you're missing us?"

Yes, I'm with it enough to know he's misquoting some of Taylor Swift's lyrics my way. Trust me, the Swifties that come to my games LOVE it when I'm on the ice. Only because they always play "Back to December" when I come out. I can only imagine how often it'll get airtime in the arena now, once I am back.

"Funny thing happened on the way to the NHL. I realized that you guys were the wind beneath my wings, and this little birdie can't fly without ya."

Henry groans. "Oh, good one. While it's great to hear your voice, the dad jokes are gonna get old quick." He laughs. "So, you're back for the last few games. Are you ready?"

"I'm still waiting for the exact days I need to be there, but it sounds like it's any day."

"Well, if you need a place to crash, mi casa is su casa. I've already made up the spare bedroom for you."

"Really?"

"In total anticipation," he teases. "No. I actually haven't, but I will. You sold your old place, right?"

"Yeah. You know, when I lit the fire on the bridge as I left town? I got rid of that, too."

"It wasn't so much a fire as a Molotov cocktail thrown at your family, okay?"

Henry's words are like a punch to the gut, but he's right. When I left the Renegades, I left fast. The offer had come in from the Blades at a time when I wasn't being played as often as I thought I should have been. I had a case of "I'm the star-itis" and it was bad. I should have, could have, and would have...all the things. I'd barely consulted Travis, which he wasn't that happy about. Instead, I just said yes and left it for him to coordinate.

"As much as I hate hearing that, you're right." Sighing, I press the phone tight against my ear. "I'm sorry, Henry. I really am. I made a huge mistake."

"You sure did. And while I'm okay with things now because we've talked, you know you have a little bit of an apology tour to do, right?"

"Yeah." It makes me sick to my stomach, but I know it. As I'm digesting the thought, a tone sounds in my ear. Pulling the phone away to look at my screen, it's Henry requesting a video call.

"Are you doing that on purpose?" I ask, bewildered.

"Just accept the video call so we can speak man-to-man, December," he orders.

I do as I'm told, and Henry's face fills the screen. He lifts his coffee mug and grins as he pulls the camera back, and a few of my old teammates are suddenly in the frame.

"Figured if you want to get started, now is the perfect time," Henry half-purrs, half-chokes as he laughs.

The guys he's with are the ones I left high and dry. I never even told them I was unhappy, I just bailed. There's Dixon, who is the best goalie I've ever met, and Campbell and Sawyer, who are cousins that play left and right wing—and because they grew up together, they play like they share a body and a brain. It's magical. Standing in the way back is Ollie, another defenseman who works side by side with Henry on the ice.

"Hey, fellas," I say, trying not to be weird and bite my lip, but this whole thing makes me nervous. "I want you guys to know my plan was to reach out to you all individually and talk."

Ollie pushes his way to the front, crosses his arms, and cocks his head to one side. "Oh, really? How come I didn't get a message?"

"Yeah," Dixon echoes, his head coming into frame. There's a juggling of the phone and I think he's taken it from Henry. "Where was my text that we needed to talk?"

I'm struggling for words when Ollie's face breaks into a huge grin and Dixon smacks his arm.

"You know we forgive you," Dixon musters. "If a team dangled that much money in front of me to jump ship, I might do the same thing."

"Bite your tongue," someone growls—that someone being Sawyer, who gets a look of approval from Campbell standing right beside him. Like conjoined twins, these two. "None of us get to do that. Ever."

He then looks directly at the camera and it feels like he's looking right into my soul. "You hear that, December? If you come back, don't pull this kind of thing again or we will hurt you."

"That's pretty cut and dry." Shaking my head, I run my fingers through my hair. There's a bead of perspiration on my upper lip that stems fully from the duress this call is giving me, but I need to take accountability. "I thought you would all be a little harsher than this, to be honest."

"Well, you're not here yet." Henry laughs. "The payback will come on the ice. Also, Leon is gonna be a little disappointed he's not playing center anymore, so we'll let him deal with you on his terms."

Leon Tully. As the Southern women like to say: bless his

heart. He wanted that position so badly and I all but threw it at him. Now here I am coming back to take it from his grasp. He's probably going to kill me, but I'll deal with it.

"That's fine. I'll talk to Leon." I take a deep breath and square my shoulders. "And Coach?"

"Ohhh," all the guys say at once, Ollie and Dixon both making faces. The cousins step away, but the other three stay in frame and shake their heads.

"You're going to need to do some serious butt-kissing there," Ollie says, nodding his head.

"So many smooches," Dixon agrees. "He was furious for months after you left."

"So furious," Ollie continues. "He had a picture of you on the wall in his office and he'd go by and flick it." Ollie holds his fingers in the air and mimes flicking something. "Like that. Flick, flick, flickity-flick."

"I got flicked?" Cringing, I know what that means. A flick is reserved for when he's really mad, because our coach? He's literally the nicest guy out there. "Coach Masters was mad enough he flicked me? Huh."

Ben Masters, nice guy. Used to be a coach for a high school hockey team that was known for their winning under his leadership, because he rolled in and made them a family. He took that high school team to great heights, and then somehow got hired by the Renegades. He brought that family feel to our gang and everything changed. We all changed when he became our coach—and I like to think I changed for the better, but the way I left makes me realize I still have a lot to learn.

And thus, clean up.

"Are you going to talk to him soon?" Henry asks.

Nodding, I lean forward and rest my elbow on my knee. "For sure. I'll try to get a hold of him as soon as I can."

"Try calling his assistant and getting her to put you on his schedule," Ollie suggests. "Her name is Anna and she's awesome."

"You only say that because you have a low-key crush on her." Dixon chortles, nudging Ollie in the ribs.

"So what? Shut up," Ollie says, taking a play swipe at Dixon. There's another juggle of the phone, and soon Henry's back and solo. With a huge grin on his face.

"That went well, huh?"

"You tricked me."

"I feel like it was a 'let's rip the Band-Aid off' situation."

"You're right," I say with a shrug. "And I'm glad I did it. Thank you."

"Of course. And I mean it about the spare bedroom. It's yours. You don't need to try to find a place or get a hotel. Just come stay here while we get you acclimated again, okay?"

"Thanks, Henry. I mean it."

"I know you'd do the same for me."

He's right.

We disconnect and I sit on the bench, watching as the local men's team hits the ice to do a few drills. Seeing them as they laugh and joke while they work together on drills as they warm up reminds me of the guys on the Renegades. I'm grateful for their forgiveness, and I know that just because they were easy on me today doesn't mean they'll be easy on me when I'm back. And I deserve what they're going to dish out, but I'll take it. Because it's family.

I'm filled with a feeling of hope and excitement for the first time in a very long time. Scanning the arena, I watch a few women climb into the stands, probably the wives or girlfriends of some of the players here to cheer them on. To be supportive. I want that. I want to look up into the stands and see someone there, cheering me on, reminding me I have someone on my side.

There's only one person I can see being that person to me. Grabbing my phone again, I grin. The one I want to talk to and share what just happened with, the one who I hope to see sitting in the stands for me, one day...I know she's out there.

My heart ridiculously full, I text Riley to see if she's home.

FOURTEEN

Riley

The late afternoon sun spills onto the floor of my apartment. I've spent the day cleaning—it's a nervous habit but a good one. It's the day before my dinner and there's nothing left for me to do except wait.

I'm about to sit down when I notice a pile of leaves on my balcony. Rolling my eyes, I know I need to get rid of it now or it'll make me crazy. Sliding open the patio door, I grab the leaf blower from the corner where it lives and turn it on, swinging it around and pushing the leaves over the edge. Peering over the side, I watch as they float down to the ground below.

"Hey!" a voice cries out, surprised. My downstairs neighbor suddenly appears, hands on her hips. "I just swept that up."

"Sorry, Mildred," I call out. "I'll make it up to you and drop off some croissants for you and Ted later, is that okay?"

She scowls at me for a moment longer before finally nodding her head. I found out in the first few days of living here that the best way to her heart is through her stomach. Hey, if it keeps the peace, I'll keep baking.

"Fine," she snaps. "But you know, you've been loud up

there today, all that banging around and the sound of furniture scraping the floor. I'd like to have six chocolate and cinnamon this time and six strawberries and cream cheese."

"You've got a deal," I sing out as she disappears from sight. Love that she's mad because I was cleaning and trying to move furniture around. The things I do. What a people pleaser.

The knock on my door pulls my attention away from the neighbor. I smooth my hair back, stopping to check myself in the mirror before I open the door. Ever since he texted he wanted to come over, Jake has been starring in my thoughts.

When I open the door, he's already smiling. His big, perfect smile drips with a sexy ease and engulfs his whole face, smooth skin wrinkling at the corners, showing how deep his pleasure runs. How anyone can think that he's this broody, angry guy is becoming foreign to me, because all I see is the sugary sweet man who's stuck inside this muscled, ridiculously fit, hot body.

"Hi," I manage as I step back and invite him in. As soon as he crosses the threshold, he unzips his hoodie and tosses it on one of my chairs, then turns around. His T-shirt fits his chest like a snug glove, accentuating every contour and muscle beneath the fabric. His tattoos are on full display, and the urge to trace them with my fingertips fires itself up in my belly again.

Jake leans in and presses his lips to my cheek, lingering there for a moment so I get a waft of clean sheets and a heady hit of sandalwood yet again, and it takes my breath away. This man smells GOOD.

"Hey. How's your day?" he asks, and I melt. *He's asking me about my day?*

"It's been good," I say, closing the door behind me. "Except for that."

Jake stands looking down at my sofa, which is in the middle of my living room. "What happened?"

"I clean and rearrange things when I get nervous. It quells my anxiety, but today the downstairs neighbors got mad because of the noise." Crossing my arms in front of me, I incline my head in the direction of the sofa. "I was trying to move that into the next room, but it's too heavy. I got it that far, and now..." I throw my arms in the air. "It's stuck."

Jake goes over to the couch and lifts one end up like it's a feather. "It really is heavy."

"To me, but you just lifted it like it was nothing, come on," I say with a laugh.

"But I can tell it's heavy, Riley." He bends down and grabs an end. "I'll pull it and you push it, how's that?"

"I'm not going to say no." I go to the other end of the couch and point to the far wall. "I only want to move it there."

"Easy." Jake lifts his end and starts walking backward while I push mine, only I do it a little bit too hard and he stumbles. Luckily, he rights himself and we take another attempt to maneuver the oversized couch through the narrow doorway, laughter bubbling up between us as the shared task quickly turns into a lighthearted game of tug-of-war. His strong arms strain against the weight of the couch, while I push from the other side with all my might, our efforts punctuated by an occasional grunt of exertion.

With one final push, we manage to squeeze the couch through the doorway, but just as we begin to relax, the unexpected happens—Jake's foot catches on the edge of the carpet, sending him toppling backward in a spectacular display of gracelessness. Who knew big guys can't look like ballerinas when they get off-balance?

I watch in a mix of horror and amusement as his arms flail wildly about as he desperately tries to regain his balance. With a comical yelp, he disappears from my view as he lands in a heap on the floor, the couch teetering dangerously as he hits the ground.

In an instant, my laughter turns to concern. I drop my end of the couch, making sure it's not going to fall on him—like I could do much anyway—and I'm by his side in a flash. He pulls his hands away from his face and, thankfully, he's laughing. He wraps his arms around me and pulls me on top of him.

"Smooth move, huh?" he quips, flashing me a sheepish grin that melts away any lingering tension. "Were you really worried?"

"Yes!" Smacking his chest, I try to pull away, but he won't loosen his grip. I'm okay with it because I don't want to go anywhere else anyway. "What if I'd hurt you a few days before your new contract goes into effect? I'd have to deal with my brother first, then your teammates."

"Speaking of which," he says, lifting a piece of my hair and twisting it on his finger. "I spoke to them today. Well, not all of them, but a few of the guys who I really needed to talk to first."

"How did that go?"

"Better than expected." His eyes meet mine as he takes a deep breath. "The funny thing is, the only person I wanted to talk to when I hung up with them was you."

"Oh?" A heat rises to my cheeks, and I know I'm turning at least six shades of red at this very moment.

Our eyes are locked, our breath even as we stop in this moment. I realize I'm really starting to fall for this man. There's a natural draw that's happening, my body beginning to lean its way toward him. His fingertips begin to dance their way down my spine as he traces a line that fills my body with appreciation for his touch.

I press my lips together, watching him watch me as I do. Knowing I have his attention, I slowly breathe and smile, a natural instinct kicking in to lick my lips at this precise moment. His eyes widen as he drops the piece of hair his fingers had been twisting, and takes to cradling my chin between his thumb and forefinger.

From across the room, a ding sounds alerting me to a text, but I don't care. I lean over him, threading my fingers through his hair and tilting my head to the side. A rush of nerves floods my overwhelmed system, every nerve ending tingling with anticipation. His touch sends electrical signals to parts of my body that I didn't know existed. At this moment, time seems to slow down and it's just us. Here, on the floor of my apartment.

Jake's face twists and his eyes widen with surprise as he cries out, laughing. Surprised, I sit back up and look around.

"What? What just happened?"

"Becks," he manages to say as he cracks up. "He's licking my shin."

I turn around, and sure enough, my new dog has suddenly appeared and is on the floor next to Jake licking the exposed skin of his shin.

"Way to kill the vibe, Becks," I mutter as Jake sits up and pulls me in so he can hold me close to his chest. Closing my eyes, I let my fingers trip their way up his arm and then gently trace invisible lines around his biceps.

"It's fine," he whispers. "I'm not going anywhere."

Smiling, I press myself against him harder. This man is making me crazy. "So you were saying that you talked to your friends. Is everything good now?"

"It is. It's been a big day, really. Your brother served Greta a cease-and-desist order."

"Will she?"

"She needs to." His face clouds. "You know, I get it that I didn't end things the right way, but I know she only wanted to date me for what she could get out of it. She wanted the contacts and connections."

"That's gross. I know journalists who have integrity, and if they heard about the way she's been handling things with you, they'd have something to say about it."

"Most people have strong opinions about it, but because of the fact she wields a pen, which is mightier than the sword, they're nervous about rocking the boat." He shrugs. "I can't blame them. One write-up from her or a social media post can make a player the next pariah."

"It's pretty unfair, isn't it?" Becks has managed to snuggle his way in between us and is now snoring. "You would think you could get a little more retribution and not feel so cornered."

"We just have to ignore what she writes, not that it's easy when it's splashed all over the place and our fans see it." He shakes his head. "She's giving people fodder to use when we're on the ice. It doesn't get ugly all the time, but fans can be pretty mean when they want to be."

"I hate the thought of people in the stands hurling insults at you, or anyone else for that matter," I say. "But you're right. When the press gets involved and makes it public knowledge, it opens up a whole new world of hurt."

He cocks his head to the right, his eyes taking me in. "And of course, that's something you dealt with, isn't it?"

"Yeah, it's not nice finding out you're second fiddle, or probably third, because one of your friends saw it blasted on a gossip site." Closing my eyes, I shake my head like I'm shaking the heaviness of the memory away. "We would have broken up eventually—you know hindsight is twenty-twenty—but I thought he had more class than that. Scratch that; I *hoped* he had more class than that. It stung."

"Were you in love with him?" Jake asks, his tone trepidatious.

"No," I respond firmly. "I wasn't. Could I have fallen for him? Maybe. But I was always wary because of his reputation. And

Travis wasn't his biggest fan, so that was a red flag, even though he said he supported me if I chose to be with him in the end. It was the public way things went down that made me feel like a turd."

I cross my eyes and stick out my tongue, and Jake laughs. "I spoke to Travis again, and he's good with this."

"This?"

"Us."

"Us?"

"Stop it," he says with a blush rolling across his cheeks now. I love it. "You know."

"Mm-hmm," I say as I push myself up and walk over to my phone. "Pardon me, sir, but I think I have a text."

"You're trying to sidestep the conversation, are you?" he teases.

"Of course I am," I say with a wink as I look at the screen of my cell phone. Tapping a button, I read the text message from Georgie and sigh. "Oh, man."

"What's going on?"

I wave my phone in the air before tossing it back on the table. "My server for tomorrow night just dropped out. She's not feeling well and doesn't want to get anyone sick or gross them out with her coughing."

"At least she pulled out," Jake says, with hope and positivity in his voice. Which is super cute.

"True, plus I don't want Georgie getting sicker because she's doing me a favor." I chew on my thumbnail. "But this leaves me needing a server."

Jake lifts his hand in the air. "I can do it."

"Stop it. You're not here to be a server at someone's home."

"No, but it'll be fun." He grabs at my hand and tugs on it, pulling me back down to the floor with him. "You cook, I serve. Like a superhero foodie team."

"Except one of us is a hockey player by day." I chuckle. "Are you serious?"

"Deadly so. Think about it. If they happen to be hockey fans, I bet they'll get a kick out of it and it will only help whatever charity it is that your mother's working with, right? So it's a reputation thing, too."

"Oh, you're good. You're learning how to speak Mad Dog on the daily. I bet she is loving having you around."

"I hope she's not the only one," he says quietly, his hand reaching back up to caress my cheek.

I lean my weight into his hand and smile. "She's not."

Sitting here on the floor of my little home, I'm surrounded by the best things ever. Brad Pitt, Becks, and Jake. The turtle, the dog, and the hockey player. Sounds like the start of a new joke or a folk song.

The sun is starting to go down now; there's a chill in the air, but it's the best time of day. Golden hour, when the light plays on the streets and all is calm. In the few days I've had Becks, I've discovered that I like sneaking out for a walk with him at this time of day so we both get a little solitude. As he becomes one with every tree, bush, and fire hydrant (dropping off what I like to call "pee-mail"), I just clear my mind and go over what I'm grateful for. Today, it's moments like the one we're having now.

"Hey." I stand up and hold my hand out. "Let's take Becks for a walk."

"Yeah?" His eyes light up. "What about if we go and grab Posh from your parents' house?"

"Hang on." I hold up a hand in the air. For the first time, I hear their names said together and I pause. "Posh and Becks. What the...?"

"I know, right? I put it together earlier, too." He takes my hand and stands, wrapping an arm around me. "I mean, what are the chances our dogs would be suited to meet?"

"Well, who are we to keep them from one another?" Cracking up, I open the hall closet and grab Becks's leash and snap it on his collar. "It'll be good for Becks to meet Posh. He needs more socializing anyway."

Jake zips his hoodie back up as I grab my keys. When I turn around, he's holding the door open for me. There's a sense of vulnerability in his gaze this time, as if he's allowing me to see into him. Like, really see into who he is.

When I catch his eyes, he looks away shyly, his cheeks tinged with a subtle blush. But when he turns back to me, it's like a switch has flipped. He holds my gaze with unwavering intensity and its impact slams against my heart and soul, wrapping itself around me.

It's at this moment that I realize I could be in trouble. Because I'm pretty much certain I'm starting to fall in love, and fall hard, for Jake December.

And there's no going back.

FIFTEEN

Jake

The dog park seems to be quiet when we pull into the parking lot. There's only two other cars, and a quick glance around the space tells me there's only four other dogs running around with their owners.

Riley hops out of the car, opening the back door and clipping the leash on Becks while I get out with Posh in my arms. The sound of bells rings out from the driver's seat, causing Riley to duck back inside and grab her phone. She takes one look at the screen and cracks up.

"So, while you were grabbing Posh, I texted Levi," she says. "I had to know why he named him Becks."

"After David Beckham, right?"

She nods. "Totally. He said he's been obsessed with him forever, which is pretty funny." She walks a few steps ahead of us, opening the gate to the secured fenced area where we can set these hounds free. As she unclips Becks's leash, I put Posh down, and then we watch like happy parents as our kids take off down the hill, racing side by side. "Is that why you picked the name Posh?"

I shake my head. "I like fashion," I say with a shrug.

If my comment bumps her, she doesn't show it. "They were so good when they met in the yard," she murmurs.

"Neutral territory." This comes out so matter of fact, I have to go with it.

"You think?"

"That place isn't Posh's nor Becks's, so it was a totally random meeting in their eyes." Taking her elbow, I steer us to a bench nearby. It's on top of the hill, so we can look down on the whole of the park and keep an eye on these two as they run around.

"Maybe you should talk to your coach on neutral turf," she suggests, turning her body so she's facing me but keeping one eye on Becks, too.

"Don't make me regret telling you all of my secrets," I cajole, but I like hearing her opinion about what I can or can't do. On the ride over, I'd touched on the last conversation I needed to have before I could feel good about returning to the Renegades, and it seems Riley was listening.

"I like that you trust me enough to share that with me. It's a big deal," she acknowledges, shivering. "Is it cold out here, or is it just me?"

In a flash, I've unzipped my hoodie and am throwing it around her shoulders. She doesn't have time to react before I've got her snug inside it and I'm zipping it up to her chin.

"There," I say, patting her on the head in faux condescension.

"Stop it." She laughs, pushing my hand away. I turn the tables, though, and grab hers in midair, pulling it up to my lips and kissing the back of it.

"You look good in Renegades gear."

"Why, thank you." A soft blush spreads across her cheeks. "Surely that trucker hat was some kind of slight turn-on for you the other day?"

"A little bit," I manage as I chuckle. "But I think you could wear a paper bag and I'd be smitten."

"Smitten." She cuts her eyes my way, a devilish grin playing on those soft, pink lips of hers. "You just said smitten."

"I did, didn't I?" Squeezing her hand, I lift a shoulder and let it drop. "What can I say? I'm a man who's on top of the world."

"You're a puzzle."

"But you seem to understand how to put my pieces together."

She's quiet for a moment before she turns to face me. "I want to."

"I want that, too." We sit, holding hands and watching the dogs in silence for a few minutes before she clears her throat.

"You mentioned there was a fight when you were on that team in the Everglades. What happened?"

In the past, I've avoided this question for a lot of reasons. I'm usually not willing to talk about it; I don't want it used against me and I don't want my dad to be pulled into the flames because of me and what I do. But I know that I'm safe here, with Riley. She's not going to use this against me or try to manipulate the situation in her favor.

"We had a big rivalry with the opposing team. Somehow, one of the guys found out my dad had been admitted into a psych ward." The memory of the day is still burned into my mind. "When we hit the ice, the other guys started making fun of him, calling him crazy and saying that I had a dad in the nuthouse."

"That's cruel," Riley says, pulling my hand so she's holding it in her lap. "All to get under your skin?"

"One hundred percent. And it worked. I couldn't do anything right on the ice that day, and usually it's my happy place.

I can hit the ice and everything else goes out of my head. But on this day, I only saw red." Sighing, I turn so I'm facing her. "I went after their goalie when he called him a 'nutter,' and slammed him into the back of the net. It became a full-on pileup of bodies from there, with both teams falling into a melee I'd created."

"And so you were sent to anger management."

"And so I was." A half-smile forms on my lips. "But my dad said he was proud of me. He hated that he put me in that position, but I know he couldn't help it. He'd only been diagnosed as a hoarder for a brief amount of time when he was admitted for anxiety and depression. The loss of the love of his life, and having to take on all the responsibility that she left behind, almost broke him."

"Why is that?"

"He wanted it to all be perfect, and he didn't want me to think I was missing out on anything." I cross my right leg over my left and sit back against the bench, the coolness of the metal coming through my T-shirt. "He was insistent that he show me what it was to commit to something and stick with it all the way through to the end. He did, that's for sure, but it almost killed him."

Riley holds my hand and doesn't say anything, not that she needs to. Just being able to talk about this part of my life with her feels good; I don't need her to say a word. I watch her as she scans the park, her eyes roving from one side of the green space to the other, tracking the two dogs as they run and prance together, getting along as if they'd known each other forever.

"That's weird." Riley tilts her chin in the direction of a guy at the bottom of the hill, near a separate entrance. "That guy was on his phone and it looked like he was talking to someone a moment ago, now he's got it pointed at us. Like he's taking a photo."

Squinting, I look across the field, impressed with her deductive skills. "He could just be looking at the screen?"

"It's the way he's holding it. Like, if I hold my phone, I keep it down lower. I'm not going to pull it up so it's eye level to look at the web."

"Maybe you should; it could be better for your posture."

Riley smacks my arm, which gives me a chance to wrap one of mine around her and pull her tight into my body. I rub one of her arms with my hand as I kiss the top of her head.

"Where were we?" she asks, cuddling into my chest and nuzzling against me. "You were talking about your father."

"And how commitment almost killed him," I remind her. "But it's time for a subject change. Tell me something about you."

"Well, since we're talking about commitment, I should fess up." She pulls away, taking a moment to pull her hair up into a loose bun on the top of her head.

"It must be serious if you're pulling your hair back."

"Ha," she says, flicking a hand in the air. "It's actually kind of embarrassing but..." She swallows as she turns to me, her eyes closed tight. "I've never had a serious boyfriend."

Part of me is ecstatic. The other is elated. The fact that I am sitting here right now, with this woman, who is telling me something so vulnerable speaks volumes. I'd be lying if I tried to deny that the possibility I'd be her first real boyfriend is in the cards didn't excite me.

It's just that I'm realizing I want to be the last, too.

Riley's hands fly to her face, covering her eyes. I reach out and gently pull them away, laughing, and wrap my arms around her. "That's awesome. Don't think of it as embarrassing."

"But, I'm twenty-eight. I've dated but never actually moved into relationship land."

"Why do you think that is?"

"I could say it's the guys I dated, but I'm the one who chose them. A few of them, like Todd, I knew what I was getting into. Sometimes I think I picked them because I knew it wasn't going to be forever, but a right-now kind of thing. I didn't want to feel lonely at the time, but I was okay with being alone." She shakes her head, and then slaps her hands back up to her eyes. "Does that make any sense?"

"Come here." I prod her, taking her hands off her eyes again, and this time holding them tightly in mine so she can't hide behind them. "It sounds like you were being smart. Safe. You were right to do that, it's self-preservation."

Bright aquamarine eyes send a sparkle my way as she tilts her head to one side and looks at me, smiling. "That's a better way to look at it."

"It's a matter of perspective, really. You didn't want to give away your heart, so you guarded it." Raising her hands to my lips, I kiss the backs of both, letting my mouth linger for a second too long on each one, her sigh telling me I'm on track. "Commitment is serious, and when you trust someone else enough that you want to be their person, you need to know you're both in it for the right reasons and you're in it together."

"Very true, and exactly how I see it," she says as she nods in agreement. "Which is probably why I've been so scared of it for so long. It's one of the reasons I got so close to Levi when we were in high school."

"Oh?" Can't lie, a little knife stabs at my heart, but then I remember it's Levi and I've met him. No need for jealousy.

"He knew I was uncomfortable around boys, especially when they'd hit on me. He became my go-to date as teens and we just promised we'd always be each other's backup if we needed it."

"So there was never anything that went on between the two of you?" I have to ask. It's my duty.

"No way." She giggles. "But if I do ever get married, he's a bridesmaid. And vice versa. When he finally walks down the aisle, I'm one of his groomsmen, although I guess I'd be a groomswoman?"

"Okay," I say, but it comes out a little more enthusiastic than intended.

She does a double-take and looks my way. "Wait. Were you having a moment thinking Levi was more than a friend to me? No, no!" She shudders as she cracks up. "I took you out the other day because I wanted you to have a man date."

"A man date?"

"Yes! I wanted you to meet a couple of guys who are in the same boat as you. In a position where they're in the public eye but having to be all physical and stuff, while still being very laid-back and true to themselves and their families." She shrugs a shoulder nonchalantly. "I just wanted you to make friends."

The fact that she wanted this for me? Yes, my mind is blowing up, but not like my heart.

"Thank you for that. For thinking of me."

"Of course," she says with a smile as she looks at her watch. "Oh, wow, I need to get home. I really want a good night's sleep tonight."

"That's right," I say, standing and whistling for Posh. "Let's get going and you can tell me what I need to wear for tomorrow."

"Love that," she says, only turning away from me when Becks barrels up the hill and slams into her legs, flopping at her feet and rolling onto his back. "What are you doing?"

"He's showing you he trusts you," I say, pointing to his belly. "He wouldn't be showing you that part of him unless you were in the circle of trust."

"Good boy, Becks." She ruffles his fur, then clips the leash onto his collar and stands to face me, her hand on her hip. "I like being in the circle of trust."

Stepping forward, I reach out and take her hand, gently tugging it so that she has to take a step closer to me. I lean down and place my forehead gently against hers.

I make my face twist so it's really serious. "Should I show you my belly?"

"If you want," she says, her fingertips dancing across my abs as she grins. "Good abs. Solid, but I'm sure you know that."

She pulls her hand away, and I'm laughing. Again. I don't think I've laughed as much in my life as I've done with Riley.

"What I do know is that I want to be the person who changes your mind."

She takes a step away from me and looks me up and down. "Changes my mind?"

I nod. "If I have my way, Riley Richards, I'll be your first and your last boyfriend. I want it to be that you look forward to commitment because it'll be with me. But I want you to know it's right—so I guess I need you to trust that it is first."

A shy smile creeps across her face, the ends of her lips turning upward as if they were aimed at heaven.

"Aren't you getting ahead of yourself?" she asks. "We've really only just met."

"I've always known what I know when I know it. And I know when I want something, I do everything I can to make it mine." I could stay like this with her forever, talking and laughing. "I just want a chance to be the man that you're looking for. If you'll be open to it."

She holds her hand to me and I take no time in reaching out and intertwining our fingers together. "Let's see what you've got, December."

Make no mistake about it, folks. I'm gonna win her over if it's the last thing I ever do.

SIXTEEN

Riley

Before we arrived at the residence where the private dinner was being held, I wasn't sure what I was expecting. A normal home, I guess, one with maybe a second story and a separate dining room for sure, but not a full-on McMansion.

After knocking on the front door, Jake and I are led by the butler (yes, they have a real butler answering their door), to the kitchen. And we're not taken to the regular kitchen, no—that's for the people who live here. We're shown the servants' kitchen, the room just beyond the first kitchen. It's wild.

After the butler alerts us that the host will stop in to say hello, he disappears like a wisp of smoke, leaving Jake and I staring at each other and trying not to laugh.

"They have houses like this in Sweetkiss Creek?" he says, punctuating his sentence with a low whistle. "Wow. It's huge."

I start opening doors to see what we're working with, finding the pots and pans quickly before stumbling across a closet-sized door. Flinging it open reveals the pantry and elicits a chuckle from my server for the night.

"If you're thinking what I'm thinking..." he growls, his hands wrapping around my waist.

"No!" I laugh, peeling his hands off of me, turning him around, and shoving him in the direction of the door that leads outside. "I need you to unload the rest of the things from the car, please, while I get everything started."

Throwing a wink at me over his shoulder as he leaves, I watch Jake until the door slams shut behind him. How quickly things have progressed for us in the matter of a few days, but I am wondering what's going to happen now that he's going to be headed back to River City any day.

"Hello?" a voice calls out from the hallway. When I look up, an older man, probably in his mid to late fifties, is standing in the doorway smiling. "You must be Riley. I'm John Daily."

"Mr. Daily, nice to meet you," I say, stepping forward and extending my hand. "We're really excited to be here and putting on this meal for you tonight."

"Not as thrilled as I am. Your mother sent over the menu and it looks incredible." Kind green eyes crinkle at the corner as he smiles. "It's a boys' night tonight. I have a few friends coming, and my younger brother, too."

"Okay," I say with a nod. "Sounds like a full house."

"It's a small group, but my brother...he's usually the loudest. I always feel the need to warn folks. He's a bit of a loudmouth."

A noise from the back door pulls our attention. Jake enters, carrying a few crates stacked on top of one another, and places them on the giant butcher's block in the middle of the kitchen.

"This is your server for the night—"

I only get this much out before John's eyes widen and he says, "Jake December?" His jaw hangs open and his eyes light up. "You're a hockey player. Are you our server?"

Jake laughs, stepping forward to shake John's hand. "I am, so go easy on me."

"Not a problem," John manages to say, even with that mouth of his still swaying in the breeze. "Wow. Boy, the guys are going to love this. Well, all except one."

"Oh?" I ask, my eyebrows hiking.

"My brother, he's a Blades fan," he says, nodding Jake's way knowingly. "Be prepared for a little harassment."

Jake waves a hand in the air. "Tonight's for charity. As long as he's nice..."

John holds his hands up in mock surrender. "I'll keep an eye on him. It's just cool that you're here. Wow. Jake December in my house."

Watching Jake, I can tell he's getting uncomfortable, but that's because I've gotten to really know him in the last few days. I kind of like the fact that I can speak a secret language with this man, and I know that when he's got his foot crossed, right in front of left, and he's threaded his arms together in front of his chest he could be feeling a touch vulnerable. I've noticed this position a few times now; around my mom, even Mandy.

John waves a hand in the air as he disappears from view, leaving us alone to get down to business. I set my rhythm and start by turning on the ovens, pulling out the chicken to get it started as well as the potatoes for the appetizer. Everything is planned out meticulously, and I know I'm ready. Pulling out my phone, I find a music app and tap until my favorite playlist comes on—Yacht Rock—and hit play.

"Hall and Oates while you cook?" Jake asks, his eyes lit from within when I look up at him.

"Got a problem with it?" I tease.

He shakes his head. "Not one bit. A little 'You make my dreams come true' is good for the soul."

I hold his stare for a moment before he clears his throat

and breaks the gaze, pulling his eyes away. "There's something I need to tell you."

"Oh?" Picking up one of the bags, I unpack the utensils I need to whip the truffle cream together, pulling them out one by one. I wave a whisk in the air. "Is it good news?"

"Depends," he says slowly as he dips a hand into the bag to help, pulling out a pair of wooden spoons. "I'm leaving in two days. Your brother texted when we were on the way over. They want me there for practice by the end of the week so I can play the home game this weekend."

"Oh." I knew it was coming, so I shouldn't be surprised, but I'm not ready. Not yet. I feel like this world that we're in here, in Sweetkiss Creek, is special. It's ours and only ours. Sure, he has this reporter who's bothering him and I've got Todd, but we also have each other to talk to and so much more to learn yet about one another. I'm not ready for this part of us to be broken and shared. Not yet.

This is why I can feel a splash of cold water, an inkling of worry, that maybe we're only good here away from the crowds and the people, away from reality. A lot can happen once he goes back to his real life, which is nowhere near what I have in Sweetkiss Creek.

"Hey," Jake whispers, standing beside me and wrapping an arm around my waist. "What's that look for?"

Shrugging, I glance his way as I pull out a clove of garlic and start mincing. "It's fine. I'm fine."

"No, you're not," he says. "You don't think because I'm going back that this will stop, do you? This," he says, pointing back and forth from me to himself. "Because I don't want this to stop. I want to figure it out."

Placing my knife down, I pause what I'm doing and stare at my hands. "Really?"

Jake takes my hands in his. "Really. Let's not look at this as goodbye because it's not that dramatic."

A noise from outside the kitchen door reminds us that we're not alone.

"This is also a conversation we should wait to have after tonight," I say, plastering a smile on my face as I get back to the business at hand. "Right now, I need you to go find that butler and ask him what dishes they want us to use, then get to stepping and make sure the dining room is set up. Got it?"

"Yes, chef," Jake growls, winking. "I like it when you're bossy."

Giggling, I wait until he's out of the room before I let the smile slide off my lips. I hear his words, I know he means what he's saying, but I've also been down this road before. One where someone makes a promise to me and I hold out, hoping to see it to fruition. Todd was a different story, a different man than Jake, and I know that. But why is it so hard to put that past hurt behind me this time?

Swallowing the small lump in my throat, I put my head down and do the one thing I know I can do well right now— lose myself in my cooking. We can deal with this other stuff later.

"They are loving every bite," Jake says as he walks back into the kitchen for the third time in ten minutes, holding another empty wine bottle. "They're also loving my hockey stories and"—he dangles the empty bottle in the air before tossing it in the recycling bin—"they're going through the wine like it's water and they've been in the desert for days."

"I'm so glad it's you who's here tonight," I acknowledge, plating the last dessert that will go out. "What a night! Everything has flowed really well, huh?"

"They love it. I heard John say he's going to talk to you about doing another private dinner for him in a few weeks.

Did you know he's the owner of that local rideshare app, Hitch?"

"You're kidding," I say, slapping my hand over my mouth in an attempt to choke down my laugh. "That's hilarious."

"In a roundabout way, we should thank him for introducing us." Jake winks as he grabs a couple of the desert platters and hoists them in the air. "Can I take these out now? A couple of these guys need more food to soak up the booze."

I wave my hand in the direction of the kitchen door. "Go on, then, be rude not to take it out, wouldn't it?"

Smiling, I look around the kitchen and let out a long, slow breath of air. I feel like tonight I did what I was supposed to do: I made my mom proud. And I can't wait to call her after and debrief. She's going to be thrilled to know how well it went.

There's a kerfuffle outside of the kitchen door, then the sound of a platter being dropped, clanging to the ground. As the door swings open, I look, half expecting to see Jake come through, but it's not him.

The man who enters is a bit disheveled and looks like he could be a little confused. However, as I watch his movements, I realize he's just impaired. He's probably one of the guests who's had a bit too much to drink that Jake was talking about.

"Can I help you?" I say, stepping forward and holding a hand out to help steady him.

"Pfft. I'm fine," he says, pushing his hand through his sandy-blond hair as he leans against a counter. He's tan, the kind of color that comes from being on a yacht—not a boat —in the Caribbean, and his whole demeanor screams privilege. His energy feels chaotic, and I have a weird feeling that I need to get this man out of here. "I came in to thank the chef."

"Well, you're welcome." Smiling through gritted teeth, I tell myself to relax, but my body won't let down its guard.

The man swivels his head around, taking in the kitchen. "This is where the magic happens, huh?"

"I guess you could say that...at least it was for us tonight." Stepping away from him, I turn around and grab a dish towel to start cleaning up. "As long as you guys are feeling full in your bellies and fulfilled, I've done my job."

Only when I turn back around, he's standing right on top of me, swaying.

"That's cool you brought your hockey-playing boyfriend with you," he slurs. "Didn't see that happening when I left home to come over for dinner. My brother is always full of surprises."

A quick calculation using this information, and I realize this has to be the wild-card brother John mentioned. A shudder runs across my body.

"Jake's a good guy who put his hand up to do something for charity," I explain, taking a step away from this man. Only, he doesn't get the memo and takes a step to stay in sync with my movements.

"He's a pretty boy who got kicked off his team," he says matter-of-factly. "You know, I'm a fan of the Jersey City Blades. Been to a lot of games. Never liked him being on the team."

"Well, I'll put that note in the suggestion box for next time." I keep my tone light, hoping that this guy will get the hint. Why does he think I'm the person to talk to about hockey right now? And where is Jake?

He steps closer, so close I can smell the wine on his breath. We're entering a territory that I didn't know existed for a private dinner, and I'm starting to get spooked.

"I guess when you're a hockey player, you're able to get all the chicks, huh?"

Looking into this man's sneering face, a cold chill races

through me. His intentions are unknown at the moment, and it's freaking me out.

"I don't know, but I'm sure if you want to know you can ask him yourself." I continue our dance: step away, to my right, getting some space between us as I clean up, only to have him step my way and close the gap so he's hovering beside me.

"I don't want to ask him." His tone is clipped, and when I snap my head to look at him, he grabs my wrist and pulls me hard against his body. "I'm asking you if the reason you're with this guy is because he's on a hockey team?"

There's a moment where you can act, and there's the moment you let pass, where you wait for the other person to maybe change course. You want them to right their ship and fix the boat they're on, but when you realize they're not going to do it, you have to be the one. The one to be the submarine that sinks the ship, and what this guy doesn't know is that I'm prepared to do it.

Pulling my wrists away, I snap my hand back to my side and pick up my whisk, holding it in between us. "You need to get out of this kitchen before I—"

"Before what? Before you whip me?" He wiggles his eyebrows. "I'm curious, that's all. You're just a local girl from here, right? Born and raised in Sweetkiss Creek, I bet. Guys like him get all the girls, but the rest of us mere plebs are left out here in the wind."

"Your issues need a therapist, not a chef." Using the whisk, I point toward the door, but as I do, the door flies open, bringing Jake in with it.

There's a look that crosses his face as soon as he sees me holding the whisk and backing away from this stranger, who is literally using the butcher's block to hold himself up as he mumbles on about how athletes get all the women.

"What the—" Jake says as his eyes slam into mine. "Are you okay?"

"She's fine," the man says, sauntering over to Jake. "I'm the one, apparently, with the issue."

Jake holds the door open for him, but the man has other ideas. It's like a slow-motion movie as he sidles up to Jake and, using all of his might, slams himself into him and thus slamming Jake into the door.

Any other man might have taken a swing at the drunk, but Jake stands his ground, clenching and unclenching his fists, placid and unmoving.

The impaired man looks at Jake, his gaze a bit lopsided considering he's probably seeing more than three of him at the moment. "Come on, dude, throw a swing at me."

If this is what Jake meant when he said sometimes guys want to fight him, man, do I feel for him. WOW. I want to smack this man.

But Jake's patient. He stays standing in his spot, even when the guy gets in his face and calls him a slew of expletives. It's tough to stomach it as it happens, but I also know if Jake was to even push this man away, he'd do more damage with his pinky than this guy can do with his whole body.

"I guess when you get to curl up with someone who looks like she does every night, I'd be trying to act chill, too." Unwavering, the man stumbles backward and then turns my way again. The sneer is back as he leans across the butcher block and reaches out to me. "Maybe I can play server to your chef when he's gone, sweetie?"

Like a flash of lightning, Jake latches his hand around the guy's wrist and pulls him with a rough jerk around the butcher block.

"You will NOT touch her," Jake growls.

"Get your hands off of me," he rants, spit flying from his mouth and hitting Jake's face as the door swings open behind him and John walks in.

"What's going on, Tim?" John's face is bright red as he

scans the room. I'm pretty sure it won't take him long to deduce what's going on, and I'm right. Shaking his head, he grabs Tim by the arm and looks at both Jake and me apologetically. "My younger brother is a bit of a mess. Can't handle your liquor, huh?'

Tim rolls his eyes. "Whatever."

"Tell them you're sorry," John says with authority in his voice. "You apologize now."

Tim stares at the ceiling before whipping his head, drunkenly, back and forth between me and Jake. "I am sorry."

Shaking his head, John calls out for his butler, who arrives and takes over from Jake and ushers Tim away in a matter of seconds. John turns to us, head down.

"I saw he was getting wasted but didn't think he'd push things." He looks my way. "I'm so sorry if he made you feel uncomfortable in here. I should have been more on top of the situation."

"It's fine." I wipe my hands on my chef's coat and smooth back my hair. I don't want to think of what could have happened if Jake hadn't walked back in, but I'd like to bet on myself that I could have at least stunned him with the whisk. Which is still in my hands.

Jake, now standing beside me, puts a hand on my arm. "Are you really okay?"

"I am. Believe it or not, I'm fine. It's just so weird the way he was talking, like he knew we were a couple or thought we were one."

John shrugs. "The guy lives for the Blades, he was just mad and being ridiculous...and a stupid pain in my butt," he says. "Not that it's an excuse. Trust me, I'll be dealing with him tomorrow. You're never too old to tell on your brother to your parents, and that's what I intend to do, after I let him know my thoughts first."

"He made a few offhand comments to me when I was

serving him," Jake adds. "About making out with the locals. It was really odd."

"Again, I am sorry." John then turns his attention to me. "I hope his actions don't affect what I'm about to ask of you, but I have several business meetings lined up with investors coming into town to sit down with me. I was going to arrange for dinners out when they were here, but if you're willing—and I promise to keep my idiot brother out of the picture—will you come back to do those meals?"

Not going to lie, the thought of coming back sends a thrill of excitement through me at the same time it sends a rush of hesitation.

"Can I let you know?" I wave a hand around the room. "I really need to focus on cleaning this up right now, but I can discuss this with you further later this week."

"Sounds like a plan. And again, I'm sorry." John shoves his hands in his front pockets and turns to leave, but turns around again as he gets to the door. "Tonight was lovely. I'm sorry he ruined it."

As the door swings shut behind him, I feel Jake's arms wrap around me fully. Turning, I let myself fall into his embrace, a little bit of shock starting to sweep my system.

"Did all of that really just happen?" I manage.

Jake angles his head so he's peering down at me. "Are you really okay? He was getting pretty aggressive."

"Yes...no?" Shaking my head, I bury my face into his chest. Taking a few breaths, I stand up taller and take a step back, tilting my head to one side as I take him in. "You stood up for me."

His face twists into a puzzled expression. "Huh?"

"He went to reach for me and you grabbed his hand before I could even react." Smiling, I thread my arms around his neck and take a step closer so I'm snug against his body. "I don't think anyone has ever physically put themselves in a position to stand up for me like you just did."

"Well, I didn't want to see what was going to happen if he did touch you." Jake closes his eyes. "I could feel this fire inside of me each time he looked over at you, and when he leaned across that butcher block..."

"And we don't have to even think about what could have happened because it didn't." Standing on my tiptoes, I place my lips on his cheek and kiss the side of his face, the smoothness of his clean-shaven skin sending a flutter of fresh nerves through me. "Thank you."

As I lower myself back to the ground, his lips come down on the top of my head and he lets them linger there for a second before speaking.

"It really was weird the way he was acting, right?" Jake says as I get back to work, packing up my things.

"Completely. It's like he knows something we don't about us...if that makes sense." I laugh. "He kept putting emphasis on us being a couple, or at least alluding to that."

Jake shakes his head as my phone dings from my purse. I walk across the kitchen to retrieve it as he dries some of the dishes I've washed and starts putting them away.

"Do you think you'll still meet with John about being his chef for those dinners?"

I pull my phone out of my bag but put it down as Jake asks this. "I don't know. Tonight was great until it wasn't, and I don't ever want a repeat. Can he promise me that it won't happen again, like really? That guy *is* his brother."

"You can always put a contract together that protects you, and I'm going to insist you always have servers with you that can also be your bodyguards."

"We'll see," I say, looking at my phone. A feeling of curdled milk twists in my stomach when I see there's a text from Todd.

Pressing on the button, I look to see what he's said, but it's not much. Instead, he's forwarded a link to a post on social media with a string of question marks typed beside it. I tap on the link, and as the webpage comes to life, my jaw goes slack.

"Oh my..." Looking up, I wave my phone at Jake. "Well, I know why Tim was referring to me as your girlfriend now."

"What?" Jake's across the room and standing beside me in no time flat. "What are you looking at?"

Handing him the phone, I treat Jake to an image taken of the two of us yesterday at the dog park. We're snuggled together on the bench overlooking the park, arms wrapped around each other and laughing. It's a great picture, honestly.

"Oh," he says slowly, his shoulder slumping. "This is the side of being in the public eye that I don't like. People think they know me. Like tonight, now they may think they know you." He shakes his head. "I hate putting you in this position."

As he keeps his eyes on the photo, the weight of its impact hits me. "This changes things, huh?"

"Kind of." Jake looks at me, his big brown eyes flooded with worry. "This kind of thing can accelerate a relationship and hurt it. I don't want that to happen for us. Not when we're still trying to figure things out."

I take the phone from him, shrugging my shoulders. "As long as we stay on the same page, right?"

Then, I see it. I shouldn't have looked, but I did. For a moment, I forgot and let my eyes skim across the comment section.

The comments. UGH.

There's one that says, "Good for you, Jake! Get your happy ending!" But then there's another one that says, "You can do better than THAT." I scroll down, scanning them all, finding that there's no balance of good-to-bad ratio for comments given; they're a minefield, is what they are. And I feel like a woman obsessed.

"Hey," Jake whispers, taking the phone from my hands. "Stop it. This is one thing you can't do."

"What, look at photos posted of me online?"

"Read the comments. Those folks don't know you and yet they'll act like they do."

"Like our friend tonight."

"Exactly." He places the phone on the counter as his arms wrap around my waist. "I'm going to ask that you step away from the social media channels for the night, okay?"

Nodding my head, I let him brush his lips across mine. "I can do that."

"Good." He lets me go and gets back to work. "We have a few more things to put away, but we'll be out of here soon."

I watch as he focuses on getting everything put away, his attention fully shifted now. I can't tell if it's the fact of what almost happened here or if he's as tripped up about the photo as I am, but all I do know is that in the last thirty minutes, it feels like everything's shifted suddenly. And nothing is ever going to be the same.

I don't know if that's a good thing...or a bad one.

SEVENTEEN

Jake

itting down alone at the cafe Travis brought me to a little over a week ago, it feels like things have come full circle in a way. I take a sip of my coffee and look around, this little corner of the world becoming one of my favorite places for a variety of reasons.

As I scan the crowd, my eyes fall on the fountain where Riley and I have sat a few times talking and I get a feeling of good. That things are going to be fine, that we can make the blip of the distance that's going to be between us work. But before we do, I need to not only sit down with her and prepare her fully for what it could be like dating me, if we're going to pursue this. Especially now that she's had a bitter introduction to it thanks to Tim the jerk-head brother.

But, I also have one of my own hurdles to get over, too. Tidbits of my old life I need to right so I can step into my new one without any hesitation or baggage weighing me down. I prop up my phone so I've got the camera on me and tap the button to join the meeting. It's time for the last stop on the apology tour.

There's a whirring sound from my phone as the app

opens, and soon enough, the face of Coach Ben Masters is sternly waiting for me.

"Hey, Coach," I begin, already feeling like my stutter could sneak up on me. I worked hard to get rid of it when I was younger; it was born out of my low self-esteem as a young teen. It likes to appear when I'm super nervous, like now. "Thank you for agreeing to talk today."

"Better we do it now than the day you get in, December." He sits back and crosses his arms in front of him. "Do you want to go first or should I?"

"I will." Swallowing my anxiety, I clap my hands in front of me and lean forward. "I'm not going to mess around and give any excuses. I messed up. I saw something shiny and new, and I thought it was going to be better. I jumped ship for all the wrong reasons, including letting the way I saw myself play into it."

I can tell he wasn't expecting this by the way his arms slowly come unthreaded. And the way he leans in, too, so he's closer to the camera. Seeing this as a good sign, I press on.

"Being on the Blades taught me that if you don't have the support of your family behind you—or in this case, teammates —then you've got nothing. I was foolish to think I could jump teams and be so lucky to fall into another situation where everyone gets along and works to lift each other up." Shaking my head, I push my hair out of my face. "Boy, was I wrong."

"Right?" Coach chortles. "That team is a hot mess. They're good, but they're not connected."

"Exactly." I let out a giant breath and sit back in my chair a bit more comfortably, breaking up the croissant on the plate in front of me. Of course I'm going to have one of Riley's baked goods here. It's like she's giving me strength without being right here. "But I am sorry. I should have come to you about this before making the decision. And I didn't."

Coach cocks his head to one side, a smile playing on his lips. "So you admit you were wrong?"

"Totally."

"And you admit that you should never have left the team?"

"One hundred percent."

"Hmm." He sits back and pulls his arms back in front of his chest, crossing them. He then looks off-camera, his eyes sweeping the room he's in. "What do you guys think about that?"

Shocked, I'm floored when I hear several familiar voices chiming in, like a chorus in the background, undecipherable. In a matter of moments, half the team is behind Coach, whose face erupts with laughter.

"I guess he can come back," Ollie says. "But it's poor Leon who's going to pay the price."

"Leon will be fine, I think he likes the bench anyway," Henry jokes, giving me a thumbs-up in the camera.

Suddenly, Dixon's face fills the entire screen. "I just want to know if your new girlfriend has anything to do with you being so apologetic and nice?"

"Okay, you guys," Coach says, clapping his hands together. "Pipe down, please."

Watching the insanity in front of me, I know one thing: I can't wait to get back to this group of maniacs. Movement in front of my table pulls my focus. When I glance over, I find Levi standing in front of me and waving.

I point my phone and mouth "on a call" his way, but Ollie notices. "Are you telling your lady friend that you're busy right now? Scared to introduce us?"

"Not scared at all," I chuckle, waving Levi over and angling the phone so he's in the frame. I know Ollie is a huge fan of his, and I'm going to get a kick out of his reaction to this. "Meet my friend, Levi Porter."

Ollie's mouth all but hits the ground, as does Henry's and even Coach's.

"What?" Ollie actually squeals. "Levi Porter, you're a rock-star, man!"

"I was just listening to your podcast this morning at the gym," Henry adds. "Your focus technique on meditation as you get ready for game day is one of my favorite ways to prepare when we're playing."

"Obviously, you have some big fans here," Coach pipes in.

"Thanks." Levi laughs, a blush on his cheeks. "Right back at you guys. I saw Jake sitting here and was about to come over and bug him for a ticket to a game."

"Done," Coach says, holding both hands in the air. "We'd love to have you come and check it out."

Levi pulls out a chair and sits at my invitation, and I turn my attention back to the screen. Coach manages to scoot the others out of the frame and he picks up the phone, talking only to me.

"Look, Jake, we're good. You get back here and show me you're ready to put the hockey stick where your mouth is, and we'll be sweet." He looks at me, his eyes smiling even if his mouth isn't, and nods his head once. "I'll see you in two days on the ice at the arena for practice, got it?"

"Yes, sir," I say before disconnecting the call and turning my attention to my new table mate. "You timed that just right, made me look like a hero."

"You do that on your own." Levi taps the table as he looks up at me. "It's not my place to do this, but I know Travis wouldn't mind."

Uh-oh. I can feel the brother from another mother moment coming on with Levi. However, man to man, athlete to athlete, I can't blame him.

"Yes?" I ask.

"I probably don't need to tell you Riley's been hurt before.

I've been on the end that helps pick up the pieces. She's like a little sister to me, and to Austin, so that's all to say she's got a lot of big brothers who like protecting her."

I stay silent and nod.

"I just wanted to let you know that she means a lot to us, but we can see you make her happy." He grins. "There's no way I could have talked her into getting a dog—believe me, I've tried just like her other girlfriends have. But you come along and she's taking chances like commitment to a pet. Not like her."

I feel like I know where he's going with this, and I need to be the one to do some reassuring right now. "I don't intend to hurt her."

"No one ever *intends* to—" Levi begins, but I hold up a hand and cut him off.

"She's special to so many people and I can see why, because she's special to me now, too." I sit forward, putting both hands on the table. "She's told me about your friendship, and I know how much it means to her. Like I know how much her brother and family mean to her, and starting her own business. I see how loyal and loving she is with her friends and those she loves, and I see how big her heart is with the pets she has."

"When she really cares, that's when you start getting fat." Levi cracks up, pointing to my croissant. "So beware. She knows the way to a man's heart is through his stomach. I think she's kept all of us off her case when she was with Todd because she kept us fed."

"And that's the thing, right there," I say, tapping the table three times. "I am not Todd and I won't be."

"Good." His words are serious, but laughter dances in his eyes. "Cause you're like a penalty kick away from pain if you do anything to hurt her."

"I'm thinking that's supposed to be a warning?"

"Nah." Levi chuckles. "Just doing my duty to take care of Riley."

"Can't blame you one bit," I reply. I know my place here. Where in the past, I'd be jealous or angry for receiving this kind of talking to, this time I know something is different for me because I sat here for it and I'm okay with it. Riley is her own woman, and I know that if I want to even have a chance at being her man, I need to be the one she deserves.

We sit quietly for a second before he pushes his chair back and stands. "I will take you guys up on the chance to come see a game. Be epic to see you play now that you're back in Renegade territory."

He holds his hand out and I shake it. "Let me know when, and we'll make it happen."

With one swift nod of his head, Levi turns on his heel and walks off, leaving me alone with my thoughts.

Thoughts that keep circling back to Riley and how I want to be better for her. How since the moment I laid eyes on her, I was entranced and had to know more about her. The synchronicity of the fact that she got into my car as I was on the way to meet her brother doesn't escape me; it adds to the mystery of why and how she's landed in front of me now.

Honestly, having her in my vicinity is so special, like something to be cherished and loved, nurtured and protected. I want to rush ahead and do all things, to get to the part where I'm with her already, but I also want to drag my feet and go really slow. So slow that time will feel like it's standing still, but it won't be because it's us. Us and our journey to whatever will be.

But that's the thing. I'm a little turned around by these feelings I'm having, it's all so new to me. The feeling that I don't want to go, the feeling that being away from someone will feel like a limb is missing. The sinking feeling that swishes around inside me when I think about the fact I'm headed back to River City Virginia in a few days' time to settle back in. Granted it's going to be off-season soon, but what happens after?

Sighing, I put my head in my hands, willing myself to stop overthinking the situation. There's only one person I can discuss this with and she's at her parents' house, with our dogs, waiting for me to come back and meet her.

Standing, I throw down a ten-dollar bill for a tip—because now that I've been a server, I have a new appreciation for the job, let me tell you—and pull out my car keys.

Slowly, I make my way to the parking lot on the other side of the fountain. Everywhere I look, there are couples walking hand in hand, or sitting by the fountain, or cuddling up together and looking out over the lake. Pairs. Couples. Love. It's everywhere.

That's when it hits me. Like a punch to the gut I knew was coming, but it still takes my breath away when it happens. A slap across the face I needed to remind me of the actual luck it takes to find someone who is as intriguing and impressive as Riley Richards is to me.

I'm falling for her, and I'm falling hard.

EIGHTEEN
Riley

Standing on the back deck, the sight of two dogs tumbling together down a hill makes my heart happy. Posh had taken to Becks rather quickly, faster than I thought she would, seeing as she's a bit of a spoiled princess... but it turns out that the lady likes my tramp just right.

"This is a surprise," Mom says from behind me as she opens the patio door of the house and joins me outside. She holds up her cell phone. "Your father said you were out here and wanted to see me, but I've been stuck on the phone finalizing this week's silent auction details for Big Brothers Big Sisters."

"Frannie mentioned that to me. Did you get the Porter boys to throw in some auction items?"

"I did. But Frannie also brought up a good point, that it feels stale. Judging by the number we've got this year, I have to agree. We've only had ten tickets bought so far and we need to see at least fifty to even think about making money for the charity." She sighs, tossing the phone on the table before pulling up a chair and sitting down near me. "I've had some good feedback from the dinner you and Jake did, but—"

My hackles raise. Of course there's a but. "Yes?"

"I also heard that you were put in a horrible position by the host's younger brother." She tilts her head to the side, shielding her eyes from the setting sun. "You okay?"

"I'm lucky Jake was there to intervene, not that I couldn't have handled it myself," I add with a wink.

"I don't doubt that," Mom says, rolling her eyes. "But you should never have been put in that position. Mr. Daily has sent over his heartfelt apologies and hopes you'll consider his offer to come back and talk to him about doing more private dinners at his place."

Watching my mother, she looks so put together and with it. Like small-town perfection, and she always has. She was raised in a family that was known for being active in the community, so of course when she became an adult she wanted to give back. She's juggled her causes with us kids, her marriage, and running a restaurant at who-knows-what cost for years. She was my inspiration when I stepped away from the family business and decided to sink my savings into myself and bet on me, put myself out there to be a private chef and do something unique.

She also watches me, a smile on her face as she smooths back her hair. It's pulled into a tight bun at the base of her neck, and she's wearing her mother's pearls. She always looks good in the pearls, and they're also the thing she wears when Mad Dog means business.

As I turn around to peek back at the pups, I look down at my wrist and see the orange friendship bracelet that I'd put on today, the one Georgie gave me. What did she say it meant... creativity, courage, and confidence? I run my fingers across it, calling the goddesses of all three to my side, with a special request for more confidence than anything else.

"I don't know if I want to call him," I say as I turn back

around to face my mom. "I keep thinking about what could have happened if I was alone."

"But you weren't," she says.

"This time. But what about the next?" I loop my hands in front of me, looking at the sky. "Maybe I chose wrong, maybe it's not what I'm supposed to do."

"Stop that," she coos, standing up and walking over beside me. "You're dynamic in the kitchen. Always have been. Just because one idiot pulls some whacked-out craziness because he drank too much doesn't mean you should doubt your abilities."

She takes her finger and tips my chin so we're almost nose to nose. "I don't need feedback from some local app inventor to know that my daughter is the best at what she does. You've always been like that. You put your mind to something and it's yours. So you got served up a hurdle, that is life. We're lucky that nothing more happened, but now you know to put something into place to protect you. Two servers next time."

I wrap my hand around hers and smile. "I just wanted it to go well. For both of us. I know you have your reputation, too."

"Oh, forget about that," she says, stepping away and swiping at the air with her hand. "The moment I heard what that man did, I prayed that you or Jake had knocked his lights out."

"Mother," I manage, chewing back a laugh. "You're quite the spitfire."

"Look, I'm hard on you and I'm sorry. Your father gives me grief about it all the time, but I see your potential. In fact, it's not potential—I see your talent and how good you are and how great you're going to be, 'cause that comes with age, honey," she finishes with a wink.

I can feel an embarrassed flush spreading across my cheeks. "I don't think you've ever told me I was talented, Mom."

"Really?" she asks, genuine shock registering on her features. She reaches out and pulls me into a hug. "Oh, that needs to be remedied immediately because I think that you are the most talented woman in Sweetkiss Creek. Could be because of your genes..."

Giggling, I pull away from her but only to check on the four-legged children again. Both are fine, lying in the long grass and enjoying the last rays of light as the sun goes down.

"I really want you to look at me and know I'm doing all I can to make you proud," I admit. It's hard to do, especially with Mad Dog.

"My girl," she says, cupping my face in her hands. "You make me proud every dang day. I want you to know that I may come off as being hard on you, always pushing you to be more. But maybe it's too much and I need to step back and let my baby bird fly from the nest on her own, huh?"

"Let's face it," I say. "This baby bird likes the nest, and as crazy as you make me sometimes, I like your suggestions and help. 'Cause they're yours."

"You are perfect as you are." She kisses my head and pulls me into a hug. "But, I'll always be the person who offers her help. So, the minute you don't want me weighing in any longer, I'll shut up. Deal?"

Laughing, I give her a bear hug back. "Deal." I pull away and tilt my head to the side. "I've been thinking about the fundraiser you're doing. The one with Frannie for Big Brothers Big Sisters."

"Oh? Got an idea? If so, let's hear it. I'm all ears."

"One thing you could do to shake things up for your auction," I say, putting her in my sights, "is to get locals to take part. Specifically ones who have gone through the program and have come out quite successful in their own right because of its influence."

"That's a good idea." She cocks her head to the side, deep in thought. "Who would that be?"

"The Porter boys, for a start. Levi and Austin had a 'Big Brother' who took them to a football game, and the rest is history." I'm already pulling out my phone to text her Levi's number. "I'm sending you Levi's cell. He's in town, so call and ask. He and Austin can share their experience and then do a meet and greet, maybe sign some of their donations. Pictures with the attendees...boom, you've got a fresh event."

"This is why you are my daughter," my mother sings as she leans over and kisses my cheek. "What a great idea! Thank you."

My attention is pulled away when my phone starts to ring in my hand. I don't know the number, so I send it to voicemail, turning back to my mother, who is already at the patio door, grinning.

"I need to make some calls after that brainstorm session," she says. "You know, that really is a good idea, sweetie. Rethink your position on what you want to do. You're a boss babe, as they say. You have the ideas and the skills behind it to boot. You're a double threat, and I know you're gonna go far."

"You think?"

"Of course," she exclaims. "You're a Richards and I love you."

I watch her go back inside, my heart feeling warm and full as she does. I'm still thinking about our conversation and the ease when the phone rings again in my hand. It's the same number, so this time instead of voicemail I decided to answer it. Why not? Curiosity killed the cat, not the Riley.

"Is this Riley?" a female voice says in my ear. "I'm a reporter calling from *Athletic Edge* and would love to ask you some questions."

I don't have to think twice about where I've heard of

Athletic Edge. The name Greta comes to mind, and I'm instantly filled with a rush of irritation.

"If this is Greta, I have no comment." That, and Jake is going to be here any minute, and I most certainly don't want to taint our last night hanging out together with this woman's meddling.

"Look, I've had someone in the town of Sweetkiss Creek —that's where you are, right?—get in touch to tell me that Jake was physical with them over the weekend at a private dinner."

My reaction shocks me as I fight a shudder of anger that ripples across my skin. "What?"

Even as I sit here with my mouth hanging open, I can't help but wonder if this woman, who doesn't know that I know she dated Jake, has done her journalistic due diligence and seen the photo of us together? It had ended up on the internet, all right, and gone around. I'd had all of my girlfriends text it to me the last few days asking what was going on, but I've just stayed silent for now. I need to figure it out, don't I?

"He can be aggressive. It tracks with his past, Riley. He's been linked to a fight with a teammate, and I don't know if you are aware that he was also in a fight when he was on a team in Florida. Granted it was a long time ago, but still."

"Why are you doing this?" I ask, sitting down and facing the creek again. "Genuinely, Greta, I want to know what you hope to accomplish by taking down Jake?"

The silence on the other end tells me that my words hit their target. I was always good at archery. When she doesn't respond, I keep going.

"Do you realize that the instances you are talking about, the ones you're trying to make a big deal about, are times he's had to stand up for himself or someone else? It's not just about him being aggressive or getting into a fight for fighting's sake, like the story you're trying to spin."

"I guess if I was the one making out with him, I'd come to his defense, too." If I wasn't sure she'd seen the photo, now I'm positive.

"Maybe it's because you're not the one making out with him that you're doing this?" Yeah, I'm pulling no punches here. I'm livid. "I'm gonna let you in on the secret: in Florida, he was sticking up for his dad. The man has been through hell and was in a psych ward when the opposing team started to make fun of him. Of course Jake stood up for his father, wouldn't you?"

Silence, so I continue. "The fight with Todd, from the Blades? That's a good one. Todd is a misogynistic serial dater and Jake was tired of hearing about his conquests. He asked Todd to stop being disrespectful of women and it blew up from there. Not by Jake's choosing, so maybe you need to talk to Todd about that one."

Greta inhales sharply. "I didn't know."

"For a journalist, I'm shocked at the amount of questions you don't ask," I snap. "Lastly, let's discuss this private dinner. Did Tim tell you when he called that he was drunk and trying to hit on the chef that night, who happened to be me? I bet he left out the part that his brother, the host of the meal, was horrified, and all but gave Jake permission to throw him out on his butt if he wanted to. The only reason you heard from Tim is because he's a privileged man with a lot of money who dislikes Jake because he's not on the Blades any longer."

As the last word falls out of my mouth, I stop a beat and wait for Greta's reaction. She's silent for only a moment.

"I'm only doing my job, Riley."

"You're not doing it well. Don't tear this man down because you have the time and because you think he broke your heart. Aren't you better than that?" Shaking my head, I start winding the conversation down. I want to wrap this up before Jake is back. "I have friends who are journalists and they would even say that you're giving journalism a bad name, turning it into gossip. Come on, woman. Be better."

"So, instead of talking to me, you're gonna fight fire with fire?" she asks, every word dripping with sarcasm. I should have expected as much, I guess.

"No," I respond after a pause. I make sure to speak slowly so she gets my drift. "I can't fight a fire with fire when I'm busy holding the flamethrower. If you so much as go to put this story out, I'll talk to the press myself about all of this. I know for a fact that you were served a cease-and-desist. I think in all of your digging, you may have not seen that my brother is also Jake's agent. Keep fanning those flames, Greta, and you're the one who will eventually get burned."

I press end on the call, shaking, as someone clears their throat from behind me. Spinning on my heel, my stomach lurches when I find Jake standing in the doorway, arms crossed. A lazy smile is draped on his lips, but his eyes are wide and full of surprise.

He crosses the space between us, pulling me into his arms. "You. Are. Amazing."

NINETEEN

Jake

I've had people tell me, like teachers for example, to suck it up, that I can do better. I've had coaches tell me that I'm doing a great job, don't doubt yourself. Even my father has given me a pep talk or two when I was dealing with other kids teasing me when I was growing up.

But standing front and center and witnessing someone going to bat for you is a whole other experience altogether. It's like feeling the weight of their support, each word they speak a shield against any and all doubt or criticism, and every gesture a testament to their belief in you.

When I heard her stick up for me, I can admit that it was the biggest turn-on ever.

I keep her pressed close to my chest, her arms wrapped behind me as her fingernails dance along my spine.

"I don't think anyone has ever done something like that for me," I whisper in her ear. "You protected my name when I wasn't in the room to do it myself, and it's awesome. That's like, a whole lot of inspiration for loyalty right there."

"Someone had to, she's like a feral rodent," Riley says with a laugh, all but burrowing into me. I've gotten used to pulling her into my arms anytime I've wanted to in the last few days. It's something I'm going to miss, but it's also the pink elephant in the room. We need to talk about what happens now.

"So, I think we have a conversation we need to finish," I begin. The words tumble from my mouth and already she pulls away, taking her warmth with her.

Riley threads her fingers through her hair as she walks back over to the edge of the deck, leaning over the railing. She points toward the creek. "The dogs are loving it out here. It's like they've played together since they were puppies. Posh has taken Becks under her wing and is showing him the doggie ropes."

I watch as the two dogs shuffle around some landscaping on the edge of the property, Becks running around a bush and Posh walking beside him, just staying close. Protective. I glance over at Riley and catch her grinning their way.

"Glad you got Becks?" I inquire.

"Sure am. I think he's going to be good company." She turns to face me, keeping one hand on the rail for leaning purposes. "Not that Brad Pitt isn't, but he's not so much into the 'let's cuddle and hang out' thing, you know?"

"Turtles," I say, rolling my eyes, which elicits a laugh from deep within her belly. Reaching out, I take one of her hands and intertwine my fingers through hers. "Riley. I'm leaving tomorrow morning first thing. We need to talk about what happens next."

Her shoulders hike up a few inches, rising closer to her ears than before. I keep my hand threaded with hers and resist the urge to just pull her back into my chest and hold her there.

"What happens next?" She says the words thoughtfully and slowly, turning her body away from me slightly as she casts her eyes out over the horizon. She shrugs her shoulders as a breeze flits over us. "I wish I could see into the future because I don't know how to handle this, Jake. I only know what happened in the past when I tried long distance."

"But," I say, stepping closer to her so I can push a few strands of stray hair out of her face, "I'm not him, and you know that."

"That I do," she says with a smile, letting the weight of her head rest in the palm of my hand. "I worry that we've only known each other for what, maybe ten days? I feel like here we're in a bubble."

"A bubble?"

"Like a love bubble." My eyebrows shoot up, and she holds up her hand. "Not that I'm saying..."

"Oh, you said it. You are in love with me."

Riley laughs and smacks at my hands, pulling away playfully. "No. I promise you, I'll tell you when I love you. You know, if you don't tell me first, that is."

"You think I'll tell you first?"

She pushes her hair back behind an ear as she places her hands on her hips and winks. "I guess we'll have to wait and see."

"What if I don't want to wait?"

"Well, I'm going to insist that you do," she says. "Because if you tell me now that you love me, I won't believe it."

"Because it's only been ten days."

"Yep." She treats me to a half-smile before she wags a finger in my direction. "I've thought a lot about this, you know."

"Oh?" I want to tell her that I have too, that I think about the fact that in the short amount of time we've known each other, she's gotten me quicker and on a deeper level than most people who have known me for years. I think about the first time I laid eyes on her and the way my heart slammed in my chest when I looked into her eyes. I knew at that moment I was gone.

What I really want to say is that I think about what a future would be like with her in it, because the thought of a future without her is too much for me to even bear right now. Not when I feel like everything is finally getting onto the right track for me for once in my life.

"Yes," she continues. "I'm just starting to do things on my own, like the private dinner, and I finally don't feel like a lost kid who just works for her parents because they have a cafe. I feel like there are possibilities for me to choose from. I'm not sure what any of it means right now, and it's all super confusing."

She wraps her hand around mine. "I was already in this place, trying to figure things out, when you entered from stage right. And I wasn't expecting you. Not one bit, not at all! And you are the most beautiful accident that has ever happened to me."

Pulling her hand to my lips, I kiss the back of it lightly, letting my lips linger there for a moment to savor the sweet taste of her skin. "Don't think I've been called beautiful before."

"Well, you are," she manages, her tone hushed. "And kind, gentle, and funny. It also helps that you have enough morals that you actually knocked the what's it outta my ex before we even met."

She smirks, I shrug. "What can I say? Does it mean we're like that trope in fantasy books...fated mates?"

"Could be," she responds, leaning into me. "Not sure if we qualify for insta-love?"

"Is that a trope, too?" I ask, and she nods.

"It is. When the two main characters in a book see each other and fall right away for the other. It's basically love at first sight."

I nod my head slowly. "I mean, in a way I had a little bit of insta-love for you when we met..."

"No you didn't!" she says, play smacking me again. "You can't. People don't have that happen. It's only in the movies."

"Maybe. But what if it isn't?" Still holding her in my arms, I look down at her, and using my thumb and forefinger I tilt her chin up to face me. "How do you know?"

The way her lips beckon to me, I have no words. Softly, I place mine on hers and taste her, savoring the moment. It's a kiss that begs her to stay with me, by my side, but a kiss that's also respectful because I want her to be happy.

There's a senselessness to this kiss, making me lose my mind as I let my hands slide up her arms, then back down as I wrap them around her waist and pull her tight against me. Saying we fit like a glove is trite, and a puzzle piece is overused. It's like we snap together.

She slows things down, and remembering we're on the deck of her childhood home, I follow her lead.

"We're not doing a good job of figuring things out," she murmurs, her hands sliding underneath my shirt again as she runs her fingers up and down my back.

"No, we're not," I say, stepping away and grabbing the bag I had brought out onto the deck with me. "I have something for you."

"A gift?"

"Yep."

I hand her the bag and watch as she tucks her hand inside and pulls out a box of candy rings, all watermelon flavored.

"For me?" She holds the box in the air and giggles. "This is awesome, thank you."

I point to the writing on the box. "There's only ten in there."

"One for every day we've known each other."

"Maybe. Or it's just what I could get." I shrug. "I have more, and I'm holding them hostage."

"Really?"

"Yep. You get your next batch when I see you again." Did I really find a local supplier and almost buy them out of candy rings so I could try to blackmail...let's change that...*lure* her to me with sugar? Yes. Yes I did. I have enough candy rings now that I had to arrange for storage, thank you very much.

"So it's a bribe to get me to come see you?"

"One hundred percent. And I've got more coming your way, just you wait and see."

"This isn't the last of them?" she asks, incredulous.

"Oh no, it's not." Does this woman play me for a fool? I know what it's going to take to get her to be mine and I'm prepared for this journey. "Look, I understand how much it would have hurt to have found out about Todd the way you did, in a photo online. And now you meet me, and part of what comes with my world is knowing that a part of you is opened up to the public eye as well."

She doesn't say anything, she just nods her head.

"Riley Richards, I am prepared to make mountains move for you. I want to be the man who you know you can rely on, the one who you think of first every morning and the one you want to say goodnight to before you fall asleep. I want to be the man who inspires you as much as you inspire me." Wrapping my arms around her, I stare deep into her eyes. "I want this from you because you have all of this from me and you don't know it."

"What do you mean?"

"You're the first person I think about when my eyes snap open." My eyes then rock over to the backyard where Posh still plays with Becks, then back to Riley. "Posh is second now, and she doesn't like it at all, but she'll get used to it."

A soft blush makes its way across her features, sending a thrill through my body.

"Riley, come to my first game back in two days. Please. I'd love to have you in the stands for that first night back."

Riley opens her mouth, then closes it, hesitating. "I can't."

Two words I wasn't prepared to hear. "What?"

She shakes her head. "My mom's event. I told her I'd help her and it's the same night." She glances at the house where movement behind the glass doors catches my eye and I notice that her mother is busy in the kitchen making dinner. "One thing I need to do is work on cultivating a better relationship with her, and it won't help if I ditch her high and dry right after she's asked me to help her out."

I cannot fault her for this. It's family. But how do you react? I want to shake her and say that her family will always be there for her, but I know that they won't. I also know that if I want to make things work with her, I need to give her the freedom and space to do what she needs to do for herself, otherwise won't I only be getting a version of her that is half-glued together? I don't want that for her or for her family because I know what this means to them both.

Thinking back to the last-minute phone call I'd made to the assistant coach right before I came in, I could slap myself, but never mind. I'll have Travis deal with it tomorrow.

There's a look of sadness and determination on her face, and I don't want to push her. The sound of a door sliding makes us both turn, our heads swiveling toward the house.

"Hey, you two," her mother calls out, nodding toward the kitchen table behind her. "I've made a last dinner for you, Jake. Riley, I figured you were staying, so I put a plate down for you, too."

Her mother ducks back inside, leaving us alone with everything still unsaid, but a lot already laid out on the table.

"We're kind of back to square one, I guess," she mutters before turning toward the backyard and calling the dogs over.

"How about if we put a pin in this whole conversation for now and talk after the weekend?"

"The weekend?" she asks, her voice surprised.

"Yeah, I've got back-to-back games and appearances they want me to do before the season wraps. Your brother sent me an updated schedule a few hours ago, and they've got me really busy right when I get back."

"Oh," she manages, disappointment in her voice. Her eyes reflect her attitude, and something cracks in my heart. I feel like I'm doing my best to show her I want to put her first, but I don't know if she's getting it. But maybe I could do a better job of it, of showing her I care?

Becks and Posh are at our feet, dancing around as Riley starts to walk back inside. Right before she gets to the door, I grab her hand and turn her around to face me.

"Hey," I say, aware that we have an audience. "We're not done here, okay? I don't want you to think we are, but I do need you to know something before we walk inside."

"What's that?"

Slowly, I place my lips on her forehead and kiss her. "That this isn't done. I'll be free after the weekend and we'll keep talking, okay?"

Riley nods. "Sounds good. I'd like that."

She looks at me, her smile fleeting, before she walks away and opens the door to the house. She lets the dogs run in ahead of her before she steps through the doors alone, leaving me outside in the cold.

I really can't blame her for her reaction; it's as confusing to me as it is to her, but I know we're going to have to try.

I just need to find a way to get her to see she can trust me. Trust us. Not only now, but always.

Because I don't want a life where she's not in it.

TWENTY

Riley

I woke up on the day Jake left town with an ache inside of me that couldn't be filled. I even tried to eat one of the candy rings he gave me and it made my stomach turn. In fact, I've barely managed much down my throat today, but I'm here, with my mom, at the event space getting her set up for tomorrow night's fundraiser.

"What time is Levi stopping by with those bales of hay?" she calls out as she crosses the room. She'd commandeered a church hall in town for the event, proud of herself for getting them to donate it and spare her a rental fee. "I want to get them in here first so we're not tracking in hay once we get the other parts set up."

I look at my phone. "The last time he texted me was about twenty minutes ago, and he was on the outskirts of town. He'll be here soon."

"That was a nice dinner last night," my mother says as she sashays by me with a load of tablecloths in her arms. She walks over to where several long tables have been set up and begins draping them, signaling for me to come help her. "Did you get to say goodbye to Jake?"

"Sure did," I sing out, not wanting to talk about it. Not that we had a chance to say a proper goodbye, not with my parents hanging around after dinner and the arrival of their neighbors who decided to stop by, so of course there was dessert and more talking. I'd finally left close to eleven knowing that Jake needed to pack and get to bed if he wanted to be on the road by six this morning.

"And, will you see him again?" she asks, not subtly. I shrug in response. "You two were outside talking for quite a while."

"That we were," I acknowledge, taking some of the fabric and lifting it across the table, letting it settle in place. "He's a very interesting man."

"I'll say. Hot, too."

"Mom!"

"I'm old, not dead."

Her statement reminds me of Jake and the first time I'd seen him in my room. "I love how Posh does that thing with her little legs, where she sticks them out straight and makes you think she's dead."

Mom laughs, throwing her head back. "And how Jake would say that she's not dead, just dramatic? Too cute. That man and his dog were a delight."

I snort and she sighs. "What did I do now?"

"You said delight. It's cute."

"Well, he was. He's the kind of guy I wouldn't mind having come back around, if you know what I mean."

"I don't have any idea what you're saying," I respond, ducking the insinuation.

"Stop it, you are not stupid," she snaps, playfully but still a snap. "Look, I saw the sparks fly between you two. All I can say is keep your heart open."

I open my mouth to say something, but she shoots me a look that tells me to shut it, which I do and right in time. A moment later, the front doors fly open and Levi comes walking in with Georgie right behind him.

"Hi," I say, looking at the two of them. "What are you two doing together?"

"Ran into her outside," Levi says, giving me a quick hug before heading over to my mom. "Hey, Mrs. Richards, just point to where you want me to drop these bales, and I'll get it done."

I watch with Georgie as Hurricane Levi combines forces with Mad Dog and the two of them set about getting hay bales organized. Giggling, I turn to my friend.

"You here to help, too?"

She nods. "I saw your mom earlier and she mentioned you would be here setting up. She also said you suggested that Levi and Austin host tomorrow night and share their stories for the fundraiser?"

"It seems like a smart idea to me." I pick up a tablecloth and start draping the next table. "A silent auction is one thing, but having it a special VIP experience is another."

"It's a great idea. In fact..." She points over her shoulder. "I spent some time this morning looking up authors who were in Big Brothers Big Sisters and I found a few. So I pulled their books off the shelves to donate. I was telling Levi about it, and he's going to use them as spot prizes for giveaways during their talk."

"That is epic," I say, fighting the urge to cheer loudly. "Mom is going to love it." I look around the room and spy Levi solo setting up hay bales, but my mother is nowhere to be seen. "Where did she go anyway?"

A voice behind me pipes up. "I'm right behind you, silly."

Jumping, I spin around on my heel and clutch my heart. "I seriously would love to know how you do that."

"What?" She feigns surprise as she hands the phone to me. "It's your brother. He needs to talk to you."

I take the phone from her, keeping one eye on her as she walks back over to help Levi.

"Yes?"

"Am I really going to distribute a ticket for you for tomorrow's game?"

A dull thud echoes in my tummy as my eyes slam into Georgie's. "I don't know about that."

"What?"

"You heard me. Mom has an event and I told her I'd help her with it." I look around the room, a feeling of dread bubbling to the surface. "I can't leave her in the lurch after saying I'd do it."

"Riley, do you know what Jake did yesterday?"

"Um, not really. I know we said goodbye."

"You're such a ding-dong. He called the assistant coach and arranged to have something sent to you. There's a package already sitting outside your apartment door waiting for you when you go home tonight."

"How do you know?"

"Because he called me and asked me to cancel it." I start to protest, but Travis stops me. "Shush. He wanted to cancel it because he didn't want to freak you out."

"What is it?"

"He sent you a jersey. A Renegade jersey." He waits for my reaction, but I'm stunned. "One with his name on it. Oh my gosh...what does it take to get a reaction from you?"

"Well, why would he cancel it?"

"I told you," Travis mutters. "Listen to me. He's trying to show you that he wants to be there for you. This is so weird that I'm coaching my little sister about my best friend, but I feel like I need to intervene some here. You need to understand that he's showing you that he wants you to be around."

"How do you know this?" I ask, tucking the phone under

my chin as I work with Georgie to spread out the last tablecloth.

"Because I'm a guy and also because I know him. I've been his agent for a few years now, and I know how he acts when he's dating someone, and it's not like this. At all." He chuckles in my ear. "He's sent out jerseys before, but he's never sent anyone he's dated a jersey, much less one with his name on the back, and when you read the card he had the guy send with it, you'll get it even more. But I want you to trust me when I say he's head over heels."

Hearing Travis say this makes my stomach lurch. What am I doing? It's like I've been driving on a back road that's thick-as-pea-soup foggy and suddenly my fog lights work and I can see the stinking route now. If I'm going to learn to trust him fully, if we are going to make this work, it also means I need to put myself out there, too. "I need to go, Travis."

"Wait, I'm not done—" he says, but I interrupt him.

"No, like, I need to go home and see this note and I need to tell Mom I'm leaving. Yes," I say, my voice starting to get louder. "Put that ticket on hold for me, but don't tell him I'm coming, okay?"

"Okay," Travis says. "I figure you're driving up here, so I'll text you where I'm staying so you can meet me. Just let me know when you leave, okay? Otherwise I'll worry."

Disconnecting the call, I look at Georgie, whose eyes are wide. "Are you going to River City?"

"I want to, but I have to tell my mom I'm not helping her out first."

"I can fill in for you." Georgie's tone is matter-of-fact, like it's already a done deal. I look at her and find her focused on the other side of the room where my mother stands laughing with Levi. "I don't mind one bit, actually."

"Really?" I pull her into a hug. "Thank you. I need to go tell her right now and then go home to pack."

"Well, skedaddle, then," Georgie says, flicking her hands in the air. "Just call me and fill me in on all the juicy bits as soon as you can."

I mouth the words "thank you" as I sprint over to my mom. More people file into the hall, bringing chairs and a podium with them. I see her head swivel toward them so I race over to grab her before she's pulled away.

"Hey," I begin, a little breathless with excitement. "I'm outta here and it's not because I don't want to help." I nod over to where Georgie stands alone. "Georgie's going to fill in for me and be the extra pair of hands you need. I need to get on the road."

Levi grins. "You gonna go get your man?"

"I hope so." The words spill out of me with such confidence, even my mother does a double take.

"Honey, I give you permission to go and do what you need to, but I just have to ask you one thing: are you falling in love with this man?"

I don't answer, I only kiss my mom on her cheek before I say goodbye to her, then flick a wave to Levi and Georgie, who're standing with her, grinning. Hurrying, I grab my bag from where it was sitting in the corner of the room, and go.

There's only one person I want to discuss this with, and he's waiting for me in River City.

TWENTY-ONE

Jake

"Are you ready to do this, December?" Coach Masters shouts above the surrounding melee.

"Yes sir, Coach!" I shout back, staring at the rink and focusing on my role. Stepping onto the ice, the roar of the crowd washes over me, sending a shiver down my spine. A blast of frosty air bites at my cheeks, but I barely take notice as I skate out to center ice. The sound of my blades cutting into the ice is drowned out by the cacophony of cheers and chants.

We've had three periods of madness, punctuated by an overtime period that's left us tied. It's been a manic first game back considering we're also playing against my old team, the Jersey City Blades. When I realized this was going to be my first game back with the Renegades, I honestly wasn't sure how the crowd would go. The fans here are loyal to the Renegades, and they weren't too happy with me when I left.

Standing here, scanning the crowd, I know now that I didn't need to worry. I've seen signs floating around, saying things like "We're back to December!" and "He's here!" According to my teammates, they've never seen so many of my jerseys worn to the arena, with my coach telling us before the game that the merch counter sold out of them the day prior. Unheard of for River City, but it's a small welcome-back token that I appreciate more than anyone here will ever know.

I can feel the adrenaline coursing through my veins, my heart pounding in my chest. Every fiber of my being is focused on the game ahead. The rink is alive with energy, and I know that this is where I belong.

But I can't help looking around and wishing—no, praying that a certain someone would show up tonight, wearing my jersey.

The final buzzer sounds, bringing me back to the present moment and signaling the end of regulation, and tension mounts on the ice. The game is tied, and we're headed into a shootout to determine the winner. Skating back to the bench, I take a deep breath, calming my nerves.

The home team gets to pick if they go first for a shootout, and tonight we took the honors. Ollie's up first, but the Blades' goalie manages to stop him. The Blades then send out a player for their turn, but he's no match for Dixon, the Renegades' goalie and one of the best in the AHL. Henry takes his turn, getting closer but again, but his puck is blocked by their goalie. They're giving us a run for our money tonight.

The Blades then send up Todd Stillman, who is center and the guy I fought with, only now when I see him, I don't see red. Even thinking about how he was with Riley, I'm not in rage mode...because I know how she feels about him.

Also, when I found out he was going to be here tonight, I sent a bouquet of flowers to his room and told him I missed him. I know it's childish, but I couldn't resist.

The arena is silent when Todd makes his way over to Dixon and takes his shot, but I'm pretty sure we broke the record for sound and noise the instant Dixon slapped it back out of the net and across the rink.

Finally, it's my turn. I skate out to center ice, the weight of the game resting on my shoulders. I pick up the puck and start toward the goalie, and the crowd falls silent. All I can hear is the sound of my own breathing and the scrape of my skates against the ice. I deke left, then right, trying to outmaneuver their man on the net. With a quick flick of my wrist, I send the puck flying toward the net.

Time seems to slow as I watch the puck sail past the goalie and into the back of the net. No matter how many times this happens in my career, I don't think I'll get over the feeling that rushes through me when I know we've won, and this is one of those times.

The crowd erupts in cheers as my teammates rush out onto the ice to swarm me. We've won the game, and the winning point came from yours truly.

Victory courses through my veins, and I let my eyes scan the crowd. There's nothing more I want right now than to see someone I know. Anyone...

And then my eyes land on Travis.

Standing at the glass, he's wearing a Renegades sweatshirt and pumping his fist in the air screaming my name, and while I'm loving his enthusiasm, it's the figure that stands beside him who I'm enamored with.

Beside him, with her mane of dark hair flowing loosely on her shoulders, Riley claps and cheers. As her eyes slam into mine, I feel everything else around me fade away. I think someone is slapping me on the back, but I'm numb with sheer excitement.

Pointing, I motion for Riley to meet me at the entrance to the team tunnel. I glide over to the glass and meet her there, taking off my headgear. Both of us are grinning and staring at each other as I skate the length of the glass to the opening and she mimics my movements on her side, walking and navigating her way through the people milling around to the entrance.

I cannot take my eyes off of her.

As we get closer to the break in the glass, she does a spin, treating me to a full view of her in my jersey. Does my heart flipping skip several beats when I see my last name on her back? Yes, it does.

As we both arrive at the tunnel entrance, everything in me is on fire. I've been cool and chill for this game, focused and calm, but I have no patience now, and as soon as I get the opportunity I give myself permission to attack.

She's barely managed to stop and I grab her, tossing one of my gloves off and to the side as I wrap my arms around her waist and pull her toward me—while also being cautious so I don't pull her onto the ice.

"Hi," she whispers, our noses touching as I give her a squeeze. "I got your note."

Blushing, I let my eyes slide over her as I grin. "You look great in that jersey, you know."

"There are a lot of men running around here in this same outfit," she teases, that sassy tone I was introduced to sending a tiny flutter through my system. "Are you going to compliment them, too?"

"Maybe?" I say with a laugh. Can't lie. I'm beyond happy right now. I could score all of the winning points in the world for all the games and I don't think I'd feel as buoyant as I do with this woman standing in front of me. She's here. For me.

"I guess my note worked...?" I start to ask, but Travis steps beside us, putting his hand out and patting me on the back.

"Epic return, Jake! Man. So good."

"Thanks, I'm glad I'm back," I say to Travis but keep my gaze solely on Riley. "It feels good to be home with my family."

"And, we've got better news," Travis adds. "Greta emailed that she's not going to pursue any more stories about you unless they're relevant. She used a lot of word salad in the email, but the gist is that she's leaving you alone."

"Really?" I ask, pulling my eyes from Riley but only for a second. When I look back, there is laughter dancing in those sea-green eyes of hers. "I wonder who it was that convinced her to stop?"

"Would love to thank them in person," she says, winking. "I bet whoever it was is quite the spitfire."

I let my eyes drag themselves across her body again, taking in this woman wearing *my* jersey. "Yes, spitfire."

Travis's eyes bounce between us for only a moment and then he's putting his hands on his sister's shoulders. "Okay, you two, I hate to break this up but..." He inclines his head toward the tunnel and looks at me. "You need to get changed and do your press thing. There's some media waiting to talk to you and Coach about your return."

Sighing, I take off my other glove and lean down to kiss Riley on the cheek. It's chaste compared to what I'd like to do right now, but I'll keep that close to my vest for the moment.

She's here. For me. And I can't stop repeating it.

Standing up, I turn to Travis. "Can you guys meet me after?"

"I can't," Travis says, "But I'm going to drop Riley off at her hotel." He grins at both of us. "I give you permission to hang out in the lobby."

"Perfect," I say, chuckling. Threading my fingers through hers, I get the feeling that someone's watching us. I know that sounds ridiculous in a crowd of this size, but it's the intense feeling like someone is *watching* you. I let my eyes drift around the rink until they land across the ice on one sole person whose eyes are definitely watching our every move.

Hello, Todd. I see you.

Glancing back at Riley, I lean down and pull her into my body, her face breaking into a huge smile as I do, her arms threading around my neck as she stands on her tiptoes. "You're very tall in your skates."

"I can still do this," I growl, pressing my lips on hers as she responds in kind, a small groan escaping as my lips slant across her mouth. Her fingers tug at my hair as she slowly peels herself away, laughing.

"Jake, there's so many people around." She giggles.

"And I want them *all* to know that you're mine," I murmur, my lips close to her ear as I kiss the side of her face. A ripple of goosebumps appears on the side of her neck, and I know I've hit my target. I make sure to plant one last kiss right on the vulnerable flesh at the back of her neck before I start to walk away. "I'll see you soon."

It's after ten when I finally get a chance to leave the arena. As the automatic doors slide open to the hotel lobby, I swivel my head, looking around for her.

I don't have to look too hard. She's planted herself in a wingback chair by the fireplace, still wearing the jersey, and it's awesome.

I make my way over, fighting my own smile but loving the sexy one that's draped across her lips.

"You're good on the ice," she says, playfully waving the note I wrote her in the air, "but no one would ever know that this note was from you if you hadn't signed it."

There's another wingback chair in the vicinity. I slide it over so I'm facing her. "It's not like I wrote a novel."

"I highlighted some of my favorite parts," she says, unfolding it and showing it to me. Sure enough, she's used a yellow highlighter and, be still my heart, it appears that it did the trick. She flicks it in the air. "Shall I?"

"Please," I say with a wave of my hand as I sit back in the chair and wait for the show.

Riley clears her throat. "*Riley, I wish I could say that I have all the answers, that I know what's going to happen next, but clearly, if you look at my history...I don't. And I'm glad for that because I would have been prepared to meet you, and you're the sweetest surprise I've had in a long time.*"

She stops, glancing up at me and winking before she looks back at the paper. "*I know your past now, at least enough that I don't want to spook you, but I know me enough that now I know there is a you in the world, I need more. I'm committed to making us work, no matter where life takes us. I know it's scary, trust me it freaks me out, too, but I believe that facing this life together will only make us stronger.*"

"I mean every word," I whisper, leaning forward to take her free hand. I pull it to my lips and kiss it. "And I know what comes next. '*I can't promise you a future without challenges, but I can promise you that if you accept this, and me, I will always be by your side, cheering you on, supporting you, and giving you all that I am.*'"

Her eyes lock onto mine as she places the note on the table beside the chair. Her hand covers mine and we sit like this for a few minutes, lost in each other's eyes and in total silence. For the first time in a long time, I feel seen.

Her eyes rock over to where the note sits, then back to mine. "You mean every word of that, don't you?"

"Of course I do," I say, leaning closer to her, my hands resting on her thighs to balance myself. "Look, you being here is the sexiest thing I've ever seen in my life, but it's the fact that you showed up for me when I really needed you to be here that's hitting home."

"Well, I loved watching you tonight," she says, a glint in her eye. "You were incredible! The fact it came down to a shootout was nuts. I couldn't stop screaming."

"Really?" Tugging on her hands, I pull her up from her seat and over so she's sitting on my lap. I let my fingers toy with loose strands of hair, flipping them on my fingertips. "Tell me more."

She throws her head back and laughs, and I'm hit with that heady scent of gardenia and lilies again. I could smell that delicious scent forever, as long as it's attached to her.

"Should I wax poetic about the amazing move when you set up a dump and chase for the biscuit?"

"You have no idea what your words do to a man," I growl, my fingers pressing into her thigh as I trace a line down her jaw, stopping when my fingertips reach her lips. "I didn't know you knew so much about hockey."

"I don't." She grins. "I was listening to the guys around me. You can learn a lot when you just listen."

"I like listening to you," I say, my eyes sliding from hers to her soft, pink, pouty lips and back again. "Does it help sweeten things if I promise to listen to you always?"

"I just want to know that we'll stay like this."

"What do you mean?"

"Talking. Open communication. You're going to be here and I'm going to be in Sweetkiss Creek. If we're going to make this work, there's going to be some distance to contend with."

"But..." I wag a finger in the air. "It's not much when we can hop on a video chat anytime. And I promise by committing..."

Riley winces, pinching her eyes shut, but laughing. "Yes?"

"Come on," I say playfully as I continue. "Committing to talking every night. Even if it's a quick call to say goodnight, I want to be part of your everyday life and I want you to know mine."

Aquamarine eyes clash into mine as she sighs. "There's a saying that something is too good to be true. I feel like it applies here, but, I'm willing to do this. With you." She points her finger into my chest.

"Really?" I ask, wanting to jump us into the future so she can see what I see for us, knowing in my heart and soul that this is it for me. She's my endgame. There's no one else.

"You've won my heart, Jake December," she whispers as she leans her head against my chest. "It's safe to say I'm falling in love with you."

My heart races. She's falling. In love. WITH ME.

"Glad you caught up," I say, nuzzling her neck. "I think I fell in love with you the moment you landed in my car."

She giggles as I go serious. Using my thumb and forefinger, I tilt her mouth to mine so I can taste the sweetness of her lips. Everything around us falls away, and it's me, Riley, and what lies ahead. There's a tug on my bottom lip as she nibbles it, bringing her mouth back to mine in a hurried moment. The snapping of electricity between us is so intense to me I feel like we're letting off sparks, sending them soaring into the air around us announcing that this is it.

She slides her hand up my arm, her touch sending waves of heat across my skin. This woman is mine, and I'm hers. I don't want anything else because tonight I'm whole and content. I know that forever starts now and I'm ready to prove to her that I'm in this for the long haul, no matter what it takes. I'll go to the ends of the earth for her.

As I push my fingers through her hair, it dawns on me that I was fighting for her before I even knew her. Now I plan on being her protector for life. I know I'll be out on the road, but I know ways to make sure that she always knows I'm thinking of her. And I can't wait to discover new ways to show her I care. I'm gonna get creative and make sure I keep this one happy because she's a keeper.

She pulls away, tucking herself against my chest so I can rest my chin on the top of her head. I've never been so certain about anything as I am now about us. It's the moment you know. You know that "me" has become "we" and you're never going back.

Everything I do, I'll be doing for Riley.

For us.

Forever.

Epilogue
JAKE

E ver since I can remember, I have cherished summer. It's a season brimming with memories of carefree days, no school, and plenty of adventures outdoors with friends. Now I also appreciate the addition of practices to my summer routine. Staying in top form means hitting the rink during the summer months, ensuring I'm at the peak of my game when the season starts.

This year, summer has taken on a whole new meaning, though. This year, summer is the season where I'm getting married.

Whenever I glance in Riley's direction, she's right next to me, remaining perfectly motionless and attempting to stifle her laughter. I could blame the circumstances, but I'll blame Levi since he's her man of honor. He had one job. He had to get her to the church on time and he actually failed. Was I nervous? No. Anxious. I wanted this to happen, and to happen as fast as we could make it happen so she can officially be all mine.

As the minister is engaged in explaining the concept of love to our guests, I'm standing here, wanting to wrap my arms around this woman, throw her over my shoulder, and make a caveman-style escape from this room.

It's Riley, it's the wedding dress, it's the music. It's the fact that I fell in love with this woman and how lucky am I that she loves me back? And we get to spend the rest of our lives together.

Movement at our feet pulls our attention downward, the sight of Posh and Becks sitting at attention and perfectly still beside us is too much for either one of us to handle. When Henry arrived for groomsman duties, he brought us a bow tie and wedding veil to put on the pair after finding out they were going to be a part of the wedding. I've got to hand it to Riley. She's the one who worked to train these two, so they'd be cool enough to sit here today. I was worried Becks would pee on everyone's leg. So far, so good.

As the minister drones on, I lean down and put my lips as close as I can to Riley's ear. "Why Miss Richards, you look incredible today," I say with a whisper.

Those aquamarine eyes, sparkling with a thousand fireflies today, pull me in as her lips curl upward. Beautiful pink lips that are full and pouty, but in all the best ways. She turns to me and winks.

"It's Mrs. December to you. And be careful, my husband-to-be is close by."

As her gaze catches mine, I find myself staying lost in those eyes until my father nudges my elbow, passing me the ring. He is the most perfect best man ever. I think it's all because of Riley. He welcomed her with open arms as much as she and her family welcomed him.

Riley slides the ring on my finger and...I think I blacked out from excitement, because the next thing I know, the minister is saying those words I've been waiting to hear all day, "You may kiss the bride..."

When Riley leaps into my arms, as the crowd cheers, to

plant a kiss on my lips, I know we are more than right. This is everything I've ever wanted.

As the applause dies down, I step away from her. I'm aware there's a crowd of people around us. Our wedding party is enormous, between her friends and my teammates, we knew it would be a sizable group. But when I pull away and spot Georgie, as well as Riley's good friends Dylan, Etta, and Amelia, all dancing with their bouquets over their heads, I can't hold back the laughter inside. I've gotten to know this crew very well over the past year, and they are epic.

It reminds me that since I met Riley, one thing I'm doing more of these days is laugh.

Laughing. Laughing with Riley.

Laughing with my wife.

My wife. It feels good.

"Ladies and gentleman," the minister announces after he clears his throat, "may I present Mr. and Mrs. Jake December."

Riley takes my hand, but I change tactics. With one swoop of my arm, I have her hoisted over my shoulder as we go back down the aisle. Two words run through my mind.

She's. Mine.

We make it to the lobby outside of the ballroom before I set her down and pull her back into my arms. Laughing, she hands her bouquet off to Travis, who is closest to us as she threads her arms behind my neck and stands on her tiptoes to kiss my cheek.

"I'm your wife."

I can't even stand it with this woman. From the moment we met until now, she's kept me hopping. She inspires me, has opened me up to a new way of thinking and at the end of a long, tough day, she is my calming breath. The fact I've convinced her to move to River City aside, she's amazing. How does a guy like me get this lucky?

Using my forefinger, I tilt her chin until her lips are in the most kissable angle before I allow mine to press down on her mouth. This kiss is more than me saying I love you. It's more than showing her, Riley Richards December, that she has my heart in her hands. It's a kiss that says I am yours and yours only. Biting her bottom lip oh-so-gently, I follow it up with a tiny peck on her top lip, right at the center of that perfect Cupid's bow she has.

"I'm so lucky that you picked me," she says with a whisper, laying her head on my chest and letting out a giant sigh. Wrapping my arms even tighter around her waist, I hold her tight. Never letting go.

"We both know who wears the skates in the family. You chose me."

Riley giggles as the wedding photographer calls us over, reminding us we've got things to do. Holding out my hand, I look into those beautiful eyes once more.

"Ready?"

She places her hand in mine, grinning as she calls Posh and Becks to our side. "You bet I am."

This is us. A family already...and if this is how we stay, I'm good with it. As long as she's by my side, and I can keep that smile on her face always, I'm content.

Riley

"This dress is tighter than it should be," Georgie mumbles as she hops up from the dinner table. She turns and points a finger in Levi's direction. "I blame you and all of those dinners you make me go to with you now that your loyal plus one has a man."

When Levi looks at me for help, I hold my hands up in

mock surrender. "Don't look at me. You wanted a replacement, and I delivered."

"Ha," Levi says with a chuckle as he stands up with Georgie. "Lucky for you, she's a fun date to have. And one that apparently needs to go dance off her dinner."

Beside him, Georgie bobs her head. "Yes please. Before I have any cake, I need at least five songs under my belt."

I watch the pair stroll arm and arm, heads together conspiratorially as they head out to the dance floor. I've noticed a sweetness to his actions recently that I wasn't aware of before, and even though we joke that she's my 'replacement', there's something different going on there.

"Hey." Strong hands wrap around my waist as Jake pulls me over from my chair beside him onto his lap. Gotta admit, I kind of like this big, strong, man stuff. He's never whipped me over his shoulder like he did today. I'm looking forward to getting him alone later to see what other surprises he has in store for me.

"Hi." Fluttering my eyelashes, my heart skips a beat when I make him laugh. I love making this man smile. Note to self: do this every day.

"Good day, huh?" he asks, his eyes scanning the head table as he grins. I follow his gaze and don't even fight the grin creeping its way across my lips. It's a blend of our worlds; his teammates, all giants that look like they came from a Disney film, crowd around one end with his dad and Travis.

At the other end of the table are my absolute bestest friends, old and new from all parts of my life, sitting and chatting with my parents.

"It's been great, but," I snap my eyes toward where Georgie and Levi are moving to the groove on the dance floor, "you know, I think I want to aim my bouquet toss at Georgie later."

Cracking up, Jake throws his head back and laughs before

he buries his face in my neck, kissing it a few times ever so lightly. "Playing matchmaker?"

"Maybe?" I say with a shrug. As I'm spying on these two, Levi stops moving long enough to pull his phone out of his pocket. Holding up a finger that says "give me one second" to Georgie, he steps off the dance floor, leaving her alone.

A hand on my shoulder pulls my attention away, and I turn my head to find Dubs, my faithful car mechanic and Dylan's father, standing and shaking Jake's hand. I jump from my chair to hug him, and by the time I turn around, Georgie is rushing back to the table.

She points to Levi's jacket on the back of the chair beside me. "Is that all Levi brought with him?"

Nodding, I tug the coat off its perch and hand it to her, confused. "What's up?"

"He's had a call about a friend. He and his wife were in an accident and Levi was the 'in case of emergency' contact, so he has to go." She holds up the coat. "He said to tell you both he'll call you tomorrow."

I watch as she dashes away, gripping his jacket in one hand and her bouquet in the other, crossing my fingers that everything is alright. It's funny. A year ago, I would have been flying out the door to make sure Levi was okay, but there's something about how Georgie is handling things with him that tells me she's got this.

A deep voice from beside me interrupts my thoughts. "Mrs. December, there's something I want to show you," Jake says as he stands up and takes my hand. He inclines his head toward the exit doors. "Do you mind following me?"

Giggling, I let him lead me back out into the lobby of the hotel and over toward a closed door. Why on earth we're out here for anything I have no clue, especially when we have our dance coming up soon. But who am I to say no to this guy about anything?

I'm his wife. That is who I am. And wow, does that feel good to say!

Jake pins me with a smile so devilish and adorable that I melt. Like heated butter, I am liquid. The power he holds in one smoldering glance is ridiculous. He wraps one of his large hands around the handle and throws the door open. "Ta da."

I keep my hand wrapped around his as I peek inside. "It's a coat closet?"

"Yes," he chuckles, stepping inside and pulling me with him. "But it's empty. I scoped it out earlier, because you know...like the pantry in your parents' house."

A thrill rushes through me as I follow him inside the tiny space. Kicking out my leg, I make sure my foot connects with the door as it slams closed behind us. There's a small window in the room that lets in just enough light from a lamp outside the hotel so that we can see in the dark room.

"It's the perfect day," I whisper. "You made it so."

His calloused hands run along the length of my arms, his fingertips dancing across my skin. As he steps closer to me, I feel the heat of his breath as his lips come down on my neck, sliding up to the sensitive and vulnerable places that feel as if they have always been waiting, and only for him. The goose-bumps appearing on my flesh are only one piece of evidence of what this man's touch does to me.

Sighing, my body relaxes, Jake pressing me up against the wall as his lips come down across mine, enveloping me in his everything.

His scent. His warmth. His power.

His love.

I know at this moment I feel like I'm the luckiest girl in the world, and it feels so trite to say...but you know what?

I am.

I know we'll stay like this because of the foundation we've

built. We've done long distance, we made a commitment, and we built this love on patience. And we've done it well.

Jake pulls away from me and presses his forehead against mine. "Thank you."

"You're thanking me?" Cocking my head to the side, I step away so I can look at him better. "Why?"

"For saving me and working on us. Not that I was going to let you go once I met you. The fact you also want me like I want you?" He shakes his head, a tear coming to his eye. "You had my heart from the moment you got into my car, but the day you stood up for me to Greta? I was floored. No one had ever stood up for me like that."

"Well," I say as I let my finger trace a line across his jaw and up into his hairline, running my fingers through his hair, "get used to it. I'd do it again."

Jake's lips brush my forehead softly. "I never thought I'd find someone like you, much less deserve someone like you, and yet here you are...*my* wife."

Lifting a hand, I wipe the tear off his cheek and then lay my head on his chest. My big, strong, sensitive man. This is the Jake December only I get to see.

"You chose me, too," I breathe. "So we're even."

Growling, his fingers dig into my waist as he pulls my body against his. "Fine. We'll call it even for now. I've got an entire night of thanking you planned out..."

Laughing, I leap into the arms of my husband and let him hold me tight.

And it feels good.

***

Thank you so much for reading **The Art of Falling in Love with Your Brother's Best Friend**! There will be more of the River City Renegades coming THIS YEAR plus two more Sweetkiss Creek books. YAY!

The Art of Falling in Love with Your Fake Fiancé, Georgie and Levi's story, releases May this year (2024). Preorder now so it lands on your eReader the day it's live.

Thank you for reading this book and for supporting an author like me. I means the world to me that you're here.

Happy reading!

Anne xo

VIP Acknowledgement

THANK YOU

to

Tara Higgins & Terrie Romero

These two amazing people won a contest and picked out
names for two characters in this book: *Todd* and *Greta*.

Thank you so much for being such
amazing supporters.

Acknowledgments

A huge shout out to my Beta team readers: Andrea, Tara, Jane, Jan, Denice, Terrie, Shannon, and Becky. This crew is EPIC! Thank you for your behind the scenes support and encouragement. You guys are the sweetest!

To the members of my ARC team who help me spread the word about my books, and who show up each release helping me to get these book babies over the line...THANK YOU. It takes a village, and I'm always happy you're in mine!

To Glen: Yes. You will hear a lot about ice hockey for the next year or so. ;) Thank you for always listening when I ramble. I love you. And you get naming rights in the next book, too. I promise.

Here's to the Sweetheart Society!

I need to say thank you to the folks who have been a part of my Sweetheart Society (on Ream) the last few months.

Dana Greco, Leau Macy, Jennifer Yeun, Lissa Ruck, and Kaci Bonar.

Thank you for your support, y'all have been AMAZING!

About the Author

Anne Kemp is an author of romantic comedies, sweet contemporary romance, and chick lit.
She loves reading (and does it ridiculously fast, too!), gluten-free baking
(because everyone needs a hobby that makes them crazy), and finding time to binge-watch her favorite shows. She grew up in Maryland but made Los Angeles her home until she encountered her own real-life meet-cute at a friend's wedding where she ended up married to one of the groomsmen.
For real.

Anne now lives on the Kapiti Coast in New Zealand, and even though she was married at Mt. Doom, no...she doesn't have a Hobbit. However, she and her husband do have a terrier named George Clooney and a rescue pup named Charlie. When she's not writing, she's usually with them taking a long walk on the river by their home.

www.annekemp.com

Stay up-to-date on new releases, get special bonus content, and special promotions when you sign up for

Anne's newsletter.

Printed in the USA
CPSIA information can be obtained
at www.ICGtesting.com
CBHW022027210624
10451CB00041B/809

9 780473 705107